THE BISTRO BOOK OF MEAT COOKERY

A CONCISE GUIDE, WITH A SELECTION OF DELICIOUS RECIPES

WENDY SWEETSER

MARTIN BOOKS

CONTENTS

Published by Martin Books
Simon & Schuster International Group
Fitzwilliam House
32 Trumpington Street
Cambridge
CB2 1QY

First published 1988

ISBN 0 85941 453 1

Printed in Spain

AHH! BISTO . . .

Before 1910, the year in which Bisto made its first appearance in our shops, making gravy was a hit-and-miss affair of blending flour, seasoning and water with the juices of roast meat. During the late-nineteenth century, many food manufacturers had attempted to get over the problem by introducing gravy salts, gravy browning and thickening agents of various kinds; none of them, however, could come up with a complete answer. A product that would brown, season and thicken all in one operation had a ready-made market waiting for it.

James McRobert and George Patterson, from West Hartlepool, were secretary and manager of the Cerebos company, whose works at nearby Greatham produced not just Cerebos Table Salt but a whole range of food products. Legend has it that their wives raised the gravy problem one night over dinner and as a result the company's chemist, Mr Bowman, was asked to come up with a solution. He began experimenting and eventually produced a dry powder that, when mixed with water and blended with the juices in the roasting tin, made a thick, well-seasoned, rich brown gravy. The Cerebos company knew they were on to a winner, but the new product needed a winning name. By juggling various combinations of the initials of the soon-to-be-famous slogan – 'Browns, Seasons, Thickens – in One' – they arrived at the name which has been part of the English language now for 75 years: Bisto.

Bisto's arrival was announced to the world in a full-page advertisement on the front page of the *Daily Mail* on Friday, 4th February 1910. As it came to be stocked by more and more grocers, the company decided that, to do it justice, it needed a series of large colour posters in sites all over the country. It was not until 1919, though, that the Bisto Kids arrived. In the decades that followed, the two ragamuffin children who sniff ecstatically the aroma wafting from a hot pie saying 'Ahh! Bisto' have seldom been out of the public eye. Over the years, the Bisto Kids have worn many famous faces in the popular cartoons of the day, but it is the kids themselves who have really gone to the hearts of the British public. Although they disappeared for a few years in the 1960s, they were reintroduced in the early 70s, with a radical change of wardrobe. Such was the interest in the Bisto Kids, that in 1983 a nationwide search was launched to find two children who could personify the mischievous but lovable characters – two kids who knew good gravy when they sniffed it! The competition is now an annual event and the Bisto Kids of the Year do their bit towards various charity appeals and act as Bisto's ambassadors to the retail trade.

Bisto itself has maintained its leading position and no other gravy-maker can touch its popularity. In 1976, Bisto Rich Gravy Granules were launched in response to the growing demand for convenience. The British public certainly love their Bisto gravy and things look set to stay that way for many years to come!

A GUIDE TO BUYING, FREEZING AND COOKING MEAT

Buying meat

Our mothers and grandmothers only had one place to buy their family's meat: the local butcher's shop. They therefore got to know him pretty well; they sought his advice on economical cuts for sustaining weekday meals and relied on his judgement when it came to picking out a joint for the Sunday roast. It can be argued that we have much more choice today, because we can select our meat from any number of sources – the butcher's; food halls; delicatessens; cash-and-carrys; corner shops; supermarkets – rather than buying from just one place. On the other hand, we can no longer rely on the advice of a neighbourhood butcher who knows our family. Town butchers are usually busy and geared to casual customers, with no time to spend on advising them. Supermarkets are not much easier for the inexperienced meat shopper. Packs of meat are labelled with price and weight, and sometimes give a suggested method of cooking, but shelves and shelves of plastic packs can be daunting for the woman – or man – who is suddenly faced with having to buy meat on a regular basis for the first time. What do I choose? Will it be tender enough? How do I cook it? are all questions the busy butcher or the neat plastic tray can't satisfactorily answer.

If you can find a local butcher who has the time and is willing to offer the benefit of his advice, do make use of him as you'll find it well worth the time and effort. If you buy your meat from a supermarket, it only takes a basic knowledge of what to look for and a little buying experience to select exactly what you need. The real test, though, is when you come to eat the meat at home. If you find what you've bought from one shop is good, it's worth going back there in future.

Appearance

The appearance of the shop where you buy your meat is just as important as the appearance of the meat itself. Whether it's a small corner butcher's or a big self-service store, appearance will tell you a lot about the standard of the meat on sale. Are the floors, walls and shelves clean? Do the assistants look smart and are they wearing clean aprons or overalls? Does the shop smell fresh? The more the owner or manager takes pride in his shop the more attention he is likely to pay to the quality and freshness of the meat he sells.

If you are happy with the way the surroundings look, what about the meat itself? Bright-red meat may look very appealing but does not always taste better: the colour implies only that the meat has recently been cut. After cutting, meat slowly turns from red to brown, but any differences in colour will disappear once the meat is cooked. The colour of the fat will vary, according to the kind of animal, how it was bred and its age. In the chapters covering individual types of meat you will find more details of what to look for when selecting different meats.

Texture

Today, many of us favour prime cuts of meat because our busy life-styles demand quick and easy-to-cook dishes, with tenderness counting as much – if not more than – the flavour of the meat. Not so long ago, for example, mutton was a widely popular dish but now the demand is for young, tender lamb, and mutton has virtually disappeared. Tender cuts like steaks, chops or cutlets are more expensive because they are in such great demand, take virtually no time to prepare and have little or no waste. Economical cuts from an older animal will have a richer, fuller flavour, but they do require long, slow cooking to become tender. When you have time, though, do cook some of the more economical cuts designed for stewing and braising. Marvellous meals can be made from them and it makes sense to cook larger quantities than you need, thus saving fuel and freezing a meal ready for another day.

Storing meat

A good meat supplier, whether butcher or supermarket boss, will have hung his meat to improve its texture and flavour before he offers it for sale; once you have bought your meat, therefore, you only need store it at home for convenience.

Fresh meat needs to be kept in a cool place like a larder or refrigerator where the temperature is always below 18°C/60°F. An old-style larder is best because in it air can circulate freely while the meat is protected from any insects or dust, but most of us today rely on a refrigerator because modern houses rarely have built-in larders.

When you get the meat home, unpack it at once and remove any tight wrappings (particularly plastic ones) as these will cause the meat to deteriorate quickly. Wipe or wash away any excess blood from the surface and transfer the meat to a plate. Cover it loosely with foil or cling film and stand it on the top shelf of the refrigerator. Never store fresh meat next to cooked because this will allow the passage of bacteria from one to the other. When you are preparing fresh meat always wash your hands, knives or any other utensils that have been in contact with cooked meat. Similarly, never put uncooked meat on a surface where cooked meat has previously been without washing the surface first.

Most meat will keep fresh if stored correctly for 3 to 4 days but offal and mince should be cooked on the day you buy them.

Freezing meat

These days, many butchers and supermarkets sell meat in bulk at a competitive price for home freezers, in the form of a quarter-carcase of beef, half a pig or a whole lamb. These *are* good buys if your family like the cheaper cuts that will be included along with the prime ones; if they don't, such a purchase could turn out a false economy, however.

Check with your freezer manual to see how much fresh meat you can freeze at one time. If you exceed this amount you risk lowering the overall temperature of your freezer and food already in it could start to defrost. If you find you have bought more than the suggested amount, put the overflow into the refrigerator until you can add it to the freezer. Keep an eye out for special offers to top up your freezer and also use the freezer to get the maximum value out of the meat you buy. Bones from raw (not previously frozen) or cooked meat and poultry can be frozen until you have time to make stock for soup; they will keep as long as a whole joint of the same animal. Remove the livers from chicken and turkey giblets and freeze them for later use in meat loaves and pâtés; freeze any trimmings from meat for adding to stock pots and cooked dishes.

It is important that meat is wrapped properly before freezing if it is to keep in prime condition. Air trapped in frozen parcels will turn fat rancid and 'burn' the meat, making it dry and tough when cooked. Before freezing, trim away excess fat and prepare the meat for future use by cubing, tying or trussing as necessary.

Suitable wrappings for freezing meat

Heavy-duty polythene bags: for chopped or minced meat and offal. Place the meat in the bag and push out excess air before securing the neck tightly with freezer tape or a twist tie.

Aluminium foil: ideal for moulding around awkwardly shaped joints. Use heavy-duty foil unless you are only freezing the meat for a short period.

Cling film: buy the type specially made for freezer use.

Sheets of polythene, greaseproof paper or freezer tissue: can be inter-leaved between chops or burgers, making them easier to separate for cooking.

Freezer boil-in-the-bags: useful for storing single portions of cooked dishes. They can just be reheated in boiling water when needed.

Use ties, labels, tape and pens that have been designed for freezer use. Unmarked or poorly labelled packages have the disconcerting habit of all looking the same when frozen! When freezing parcels of meat, label them with the type of meat inside, its weight and the date frozen.

Freezer storage

Frozen meat deteriorates over a period of time but this is barely notice-able in the flavour and texture. The length of safe storage depends on the type of meat, the cut and the storage temperature; pork fat, for example, deteriorates more quickly than the fat of lamb or beef, reducing the length of time pork can be kept frozen. As a rough guide, uncooked beef can be kept for 12 months; veal and lamb for 9 months; pork for 6 months. Mince, sausages and offal will keep for 3 months, as will bacon joints and vacuum-packed bacon rashers. Packs of non-vacuum-sealed rashers will keep for 1 month.

Freezer-storage times are shorter for cooked meat dishes if they are to be enjoyed at their best. Casseroles can be frozen for 6 months; curries and other spicy dishes for 4 months; meat pies for 3 months; cooked ham for 2 months.

If you do store meat, either cooked or uncooked, for longer than its recommended time, it will not necessarily be inedible. Thaw it: as long as it doesn't smell strong or unpleasant, it will be fine to eat.

Thawing meat

Most meat can be cooked from frozen; however while it's easy to tell when a small cut is cooked, calculating the cooking times from frozen for larger joints can be difficult, so it's usually better to thaw them first in the refrigerator. All poultry and poultry joints and game birds *must without fail* be thawed completely before cooking, as must joints of meat that have been boned, stuffed and rolled. A microwave can be invaluable when it comes to thawing meat but it's advisable to cook the meat immediately afterwards, unless you are certain the outside edges of the meat have not become hot and started to cook while defrosting.

Tips for preparing and cooking meat

● When slicing fresh meat, cut it across the grain, that is through a cross-section of the fibres that run the length of the piece of meat. This causes the fibres to shrink as the meat cooks and makes it tender.

● Before carving a cooked joint or whole bird, cover it with foil and leave to stand for 10 to 15 minutes. This gives time for the juices to flow back into the meat, making it easier to carve and more succulent.

● A meat thermometer can take the guesswork out of deciding when a joint is cooked. Just press it into the fleshiest part and the internal temperature will register on the thermometer, indicating whether it is rare, medium or well done. If you don't have a thermometer you can do a rough check by pushing a skewer into the thickest part of the meat. If the tip of the skewer is hot when you draw it out, the meat is cooked through.

● When roasting boned, rolled meats, add an extra 5 minutes per 500 g (1 lb) to the cooking time, as the bone is no longer there to conduct the heat. Add the bone to the roasting tin for extra flavour.

A few cooking terms explained

Basting Spooning the pan juices over a joint of meat as it roasts. A joint usually needs basting every 20 minutes or so to keep the flesh moist and improve the appearance.

Braising Cooking a joint slowly in a covered container, with a small amount of liquid to form steam, first on top of the stove and then in the oven. Braising is a cooking method particularly suited to tougher cuts of meat. Originally, braising meant 'cooking in a brazier' – a pot with a special concave lid in which hot coals were heaped.

Casseroling Slowly cooking meat in the oven in a deep, covered dish. Casseroling is a way of tenderising tough cuts and the use of a close-fitting lid is essential to prevent evaporation of the cooking liquid that covers the meat.

Frying Cooking meat in either deep or shallow fat. When *deep-frying*, meat is usually coated in batter or breadcrumbs first, to protect its texture and flavour from the intense heat of the oil. Deep-frying is done in a deep pan, which is one-third to half-filled with oil or melted dripping; the fat must be brought to the correct temperature before the food is added.

Shallow-frying is done in a frying-pan with a small amount of oil or other fat, and is particularly suitable for thin slices of meat, offal, burgers, chops, bacon rashers and sausages.

In recent years, a third type of frying has been rapidly gaining in popularity: *stir-frying*. This is based on a traditional Chinese method of cooking where small, even-sized pieces of meat and vegetables are stirred in a round-based pan called a wok, with very little oil, over a high heat. This method of frying retains the food's freshness and flavour, and produces a meal very quickly. A wok is not essential; stir-frying can be done in any large, fairly deep frying-pan.

Grilling Cooking small, tender cuts of meat quickly under direct heat, or browning pre-cooked dishes. The grill needs to be pre-heated before the food is placed on a greased rack underneath it; the food is turned half-way, so it cooks evenly.

Marinating Immersing meat in an acid mixture of wine, spices, herbs and other aromatics, to help tenderise the flesh and give extra flavour.

Pot-roasting 'Roasting' a tougher cut of meat in a tightly covered pan on top of the stove or in the oven. The pan needs to be just large enough so the meat does not touch the sides and a little fat or cooking liquid is usually added for flavour.

Roasting Cooking meat in the dry heat of an oven with the addition of a little fat, if necessary. It is best suited to tender cuts of meat.

Simmering Cooking in a liquid that is kept just below boiling point (100°C/212°F).

Steaming Cooking delicate cuts of meat over a pan of simmering water. Steamers of various types can be purchased or the food can be placed on a heatproof plate over a saucepan. The food should be covered and stand well clear of the water below.

Stewing   Simmering meat in water, sauce or gravy in a pan with a tightly fitting lid. The liquid should not be allowed to boil or the meat will become tough; stewing is a method of cooking best suited to economical cuts that need long, slow simmering.

Notes

Follow either the metric or imperial measurements; don't mix the two as the proportions are *not* interchangeable.

All spoon measures given in the recipes are level.

Recipes that are suitable for freezing are marked ✳ .

Although alcohol is used in some recipes, it can be replaced with fruit juice or water if you prefer.

Bisto seasons so, except in a few cases, no extra salt and pepper is added to recipes. Check the cooked dish and season more if you wish.

BEEF

Choosing and buying beef

The finest cuts of beef are nowadays very expensive; so when a family can sit down to a traditional Sunday lunch of roast beef and Yorkshire pudding it's a meal and an occasion to make the most of! Cheaper cuts can be just as delicious, though. It is particularly important that you use a cooking method for beef that is suited to the cut you buy. Although beef is readily available through the year, British beef is most plentiful in the autumn.

Look for a fresh, slightly moist appearance. The flesh will gradually turn from bright red to a reddish-brown after the meat has been cut and exposed to the air. The fat surrounding the meat should be firm and creamy-white and any 'marbling' (flecks of fat in the meat) will keep the meat moist while it cooks.

Cuts such as silverside and brisket are sometimes sold 'salted'. This process turns the meat a greyish colour, but it will be pink when cooked.

Cuts of beef

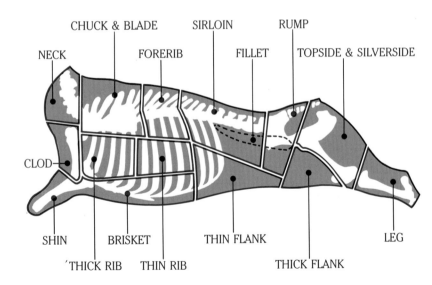

CHUCK & BLADE   SIRLOIN   RUMP

NECK   FORERIB   FILLET   TOPSIDE & SILVERSIDE

CLOD

SHIN   BRISKET   THIN FLANK   LEG

'THICK RIB   THIN RIB   THICK FLANK

Shin (foreleg) and leg (hindleg)
Lean meat, but fairly coarse in texture; the most economical cut for stewing. Suitable for stews, casseroles, soups and brawn.

Neck and clod
Usually sold in pieces for stewing and casseroling, or as economical mince.

Chuck steak
A fairly lean, good-quality, boned cut; sold for braising, stewing and pie-making.

Thick flank (top rump)
A lean cut suitable for roasting, pot-roasting and braising. When sliced it can be braised or fried.

Thin flank
Suitable for braising and stewing. Often salted and pickled. Also sold minced.

Brisket
Sold on the bone or boned and rolled. Can be braised or boiled and often sold salted.

Thin ribs and thick ribs
Usually sold boned and rolled. Braise or pot-roast.

Silverside
Traditionally sold salted for boiling. Now often sold for roasting as it is lean but needs regular basting.

Fore rib
The traditional cut for old-fashioned roast beef. Sold on the bone, or boned and rolled.

Wing rib
Popular as a roasting joint, but often sold boned and sliced as frying or grilling steaks.

Sirloin
Tender and delicious; sold for roasting with or without the fillet (the smaller 'eye' of meat on the inside of the rib bone). The fillet is also sold on its own, either whole or sliced as fillet steak. Sirloin steaks are cut from the larger 'eye' of the lean meat.

Rump
A high-quality, lean, tender cut. Sold sliced as steaks for grilling or frying.

Topside
A lean cut with little or no fat, often sold with a layer of fat tied round it. Can be roasted, but better pot-roasted.

Steaks
Slices of the most tender cuts, e.g. sirloin, fillet, rump and T-bone.

'Flash-fry' steaks
A term referring to slices from lean cuts that have been passed between knife-covered rollers; this tenderises the meat and reduces the cooking time so they can be 'flash'-(quickly) fried.

ROAST BEEF OF OLD ENGLAND

As much a part of England's national heritage as the White Cliffs of Dover and Queen Elizabeth I, roast beef with Yorkshire pudding has a special place on our dining tables. Allow about 225 g (8 oz) of meat per person if the joint has been boned, and 350 g (12 oz) per person if it hasn't. Suitable roasting joints are sirloin (either on the bone or boned and rolled), rib (on the bone or boned and rolled), topside (a lean joint that can be roasted but is better pot-roasted or braised, as it can lack flavour). Traditional accompaniments to roast beef are Yorkshire pudding, horse-radish sauce, roast potatoes, green vegetables and a rich gravy made with Bisto powder blended with the meat juices.

Wipe the joint and place in a roasting tin with the thickest layer of fat uppermost and the cut sides of the meat exposed to the heat. If the meat does not have a lot of fat add 50 g (2 oz) of beef dripping to the tin and roast the joint for 20 minutes per 500 g (1 lb) plus 20 minutes at 200°C/400°F/Gas Mark 6, basting occasionally with the pan juices. This will produce a joint that is slightly rare; adjust the time 5 minutes per 500 g (1 lb) either way, depending on how you like your meat cooked. Rare roast beef is delicious hot or cold but it is only the best cuts that are good eaten rare: cheaper cuts will be unpleasantly tough if not sufficiently cooked.

Carving beef
To carve well, it is very important to have a good-quality carving knife, with a long blade that is sharpened every time you use it, and a two-pronged carving fork, preferably with a guard to protect your hand as you carve.
Fore rib
Ask the butcher to 'chine' the back bone. After cooking, remove the back bone and run a sharp knife between the meat and the bone. Carve downwards, on to and between the rib bones.
Sirloin
Sirloin 'on the bone' is the fillet and sirloin muscles with a T-shaped bone between, and a portion of flank. When carving, loosen the meat from the bones with a sharp knife as you carve along the joint. Carve slices down to the bone, first on one side and then on the other.

CHILLI SOUFFLÉ

Serves 4   **✳** *Without topping*

If I give a party at home and decide to serve hot food, chilli con carne is one of the first dishes that springs to mind because everyone seems to enjoy it. Here I have topped it with fluffy, soufflé-style potatoes: an easy way to turn 'good old chilli' into something really quite special.

Chilli:
30 ml (2 tbsp) oil
2 large onions, sliced
1 clove of garlic, crushed
500 g (1 lb) lean minced beef
15 ml (1 tbsp) chilli powder
30 ml (2 tbsp) Bisto Powder
400 g (14 oz) can of plum tomatoes

425 g (15 oz) can of red kidney beans, drained
30 ml (2 tbsp) tomato purée
Soufflé topping:
500 g (1 lb) potatoes
30 ml (2 tbsp) milk
25 g (1 oz) butter
3 size 3 eggs, separated
Salt and pepper to taste

1. To make the chilli: heat the oil in a pan and sauté the onions until soft but not browned. Stir in the garlic and minced beef, breaking the meat up with a wooden spoon, and fry until the meat becomes evenly pale. Sprinkle over the chilli powder and cook for 1 minute; then add the Bisto Powder, tomatoes and their juice, kidney beans and tomato purée. Bring to the boil, lower the heat and simmer uncovered, for 1 hour.

2. To make the soufflé topping: peel the potatoes and cook in boiling, salted water until tender. Drain and mash. Return to the saucepan, season with salt and pepper and draw the potatoes to one side of the pan. Add the milk and warm this over the heat; then beat it into the potatoes with the butter and egg yolks.

3. Preheat the oven to 190°C/375°F/Gas Mark 5. Spoon the chilli into a 1.4-litre (2½-pint) soufflé dish. Whisk the egg whites in a clean, grease-free bowl until they stand in soft peaks. Beat 30 ml (2 tbsp) into the potatoes to soften the mixture, and then fold in the remaining egg whites. Spoon the potatoes over the chilli to cover it completely.

4. Bake for 45 minutes until golden. Serve at once with vegetables or salad.

STIR-FRIED PLUM BEEF

Serves 4

Lean, tender cuts of beef make the best stir-frys because the meat will melt in your mouth! You should be able to find cans of baby sweetcorn in your local supermarket; they only need to be drained and they are ready for stir-frying.

500 g (1 lb) sirloin, rump or fillet steak
30 ml (2 tbsp) smooth peanut butter
45 ml (3 tbsp) oil
5 ml (1 tsp) chopped root ginger
4 spring onions, trimmed and cut in
*   half lengthways*
1 red pepper, de-seeded and cut in
*   strips*

225 g (8 oz) broccoli, cut in tiny florets
396 g (14 oz) can of baby sweetcorn,
*   drained and cut in half lengthways*
30 ml (2 tbsp) soy sauce
30 ml (2 tbsp) plum jam
125 ml (5 fl oz) water
15 ml (1 tbsp) Bisto Powder
50 g (2 oz) cashew nuts, toasted

1. Trim any fat from the steak and cut it across the grain into thin strips. Mix together the peanut butter and 15 ml (1 tbsp) of the oil and toss the beef in this to coat it. Leave it to stand for 30 minutes.

2. Heat 15 ml (1 tbsp) of the oil in a wok or large frying-pan and fry the ginger and spring onions until lightly browned. Add the red pepper, broccoli and sweetcorn and stir-fry for 5 minutes. Drain the vegetables and keep warm.

3. Heat the remaining oil, add the steak and any marinade to the pan and stir-fry for 2–3 minutes until browned. Drain and keep warm with the vegetables.

4. Mix together the soy sauce, jam, water and Bisto Powder and add to the pan. Stir until the sauce bubbles and then return the beef and vegetables to the pan. Stir in the cashew nuts. Cook, stirring, for 1 minute.

5. Serve with boiled rice or egg noodles.

Stir-fried Plum Beef

FLORENTINE BEEF GRATIN

Serves 4–6   ✳ *If using fresh spinach*

A fairly grand title for a dish that would make an excellent family supper, or could be made when you have guests coming. Vermicelli is thin spaghetti; you can use this or ordinary spaghetti in the recipe. You can also use fresh instead of frozen spinach in season. Fresh spinach needs to be washed very thoroughly in lots of cold water or it will taste gritty when cooked; you will need twice as much fresh as frozen spinach as fresh loses so much bulk during cooking.

100 g (4 oz) vermicelli or spaghetti
30 ml (2 tbsp) oil
1 onion, peeled and chopped
1 clove of garlic, crushed
500 g (1 lb) lean minced beef
227 g (8 oz) can of plum tomatoes
15 ml (1 tbsp) Bisto Powder
250 ml (½ pint) cold water
30 ml (2 tbsp) tomato purée

225 g (8 oz) carrots
225 g (8 oz) cooked chopped spinach
1.25 ml (¼ tsp) ground nutmeg
Topping:
275 g (10 oz) carton of natural yogurt
1 size 3 egg
2 tomatoes, sliced
50 g (2 oz) Cheddar cheese, grated
2.5 ml (½ tsp) dry mustard

1. Cook the vermicelli or spaghetti according to the packet instructions until just tender. Drain and place in a large, shallow, ovenproof dish.

2. Heat the oil in a frying-pan and cook the onion and garlic until soft but not browned. Stir in the minced beef, breaking it up if necessary with a wooden spoon, and cook until pale and just starting to brown.

3. Add the tomatoes and their juice, the Bisto Powder, water and tomato purée. Bring to the boil, lower the heat and simmer gently, uncovered, for 30–35 minutes, stirring occasionally.

4. Peel the carrots and slice or cut them into matchstick strips. Cook in boiling, salted water until tender and then drain them.

5. Thaw the spinach if frozen, and dry it off in a pan over a very low heat until the moisture has evaporated and the spinach is quite dry. Season the spinach with the nutmeg.

6. Spoon the beef mixture over the pasta and top with the carrots and spinach.

7. In a bowl, beat together the yogurt and egg until smooth, and then spoon over the pasta mixture. Arrange the tomato slices over the top.

8. Sprinkle over the cheese and dry mustard.

9. Preheat the oven to 180°C/350°F/Gas Mark 4. Stand the dish on a baking sheet and bake it for 35–45 minutes until the cheese is bubbling and lightly browned. Serve with a green, crunchy salad.

Florentine Beef Gratin

PEPPERED STEAKS

Serves 4

20 ml (4 tsp) whole black
   peppercorns, crushed coarsely
4 rump or sirloin steaks, weighing
   about 175 g (6 oz) each
45 ml (3 tbsp) oil
50 g (2 oz) butter

60 ml (4 tbsp) brandy
15 ml (1 tbsp) Bisto Powder
125 ml (¼ pint) cold water
50 ml (2 fl oz) double cream
ground black pepper

1. Press the peppercorns on to both sides of the steaks. Heat the oil and butter in a frying-pan and when foaming add the steaks and fry for about 5 minutes each side, or longer if preferred. Remove and keep warm.
2. Add the brandy to the pan and allow it to bubble for a few seconds. Blend the Bisto Powder with the water, add to the pan and bring to the boil, stirring. Remove from the heat and stir in the cream. Season with black pepper.
3. Spoon the sauce over the steaks and serve at once with sauté potatoes, grilled tomatoes and a watercress garnish.

CHUNKY SHEPHERD'S PIE

Serves 4   ✱

30 ml (2 tbsp) oil
500 g (1 lb) braising or chuck steak,
   trimmed of fat and cut in 2.5 cm
   (1-inch) cubes
2 lamb's kidneys, cored and sliced
1 onion, chopped
2 carrots, peeled and cut into 5 mm
   (¼-inch) slices
250 ml (½ pint) gravy made with Bisto
   Rich Gravy Granules as directed

10 ml (2 tsp) Worcestershire sauce
30 ml (2 tbsp) red wine vinegar
Topping:
750 g (1½ lb) potatoes, peeled and
   boiled
25 g (1 oz) butter
1 size 3 egg, beaten
salt
15 ml (1 tbsp) sesame seeds

1. Heat the oil in a large pan and fry the beef and kidneys over a brisk heat, stirring frequently, until browned on all sides. Remove.
2. Add the onion and carrots and cook gently for 3–4 minutes. Pour in the gravy, add the Worcestershire sauce and vinegar and bring to the boil. Add the meat, cover and simmer gently for 1½ hours stirring from time to time.

Chunky Shepherd's Pie; Peppered Steaks

3. Spoon into a 1.4-litre (2½-pint) pie dish. Set aside.
4. Mash the potatoes with the butter. Beat in the egg and season with salt. Spoon the potato into a piping bag fitted with a large star nozzle and pipe rows of potato over the steak and kidney mixture. Alternatively, spoon the potato over the meat mixture and spread it out evenly with a fork.
5. Preheat the oven to 180°C/350°F/Gas Mark 4. Sprinkle with the sesame seeds. Bake on a baking sheet for 45–50 minutes until hot; brown under a grill before serving if you like.

BOILED BEEF AND CARROTS

Serves 8–10

1.4 kg (3 lb) joint of salted silverside, boned and rolled
4 cloves
8 whole black peppercorns
350 g (12 oz) carrots, peeled and halved lengthways
8 small onions, peeled and left whole

30 ml (2 tbsp) Bisto Powder
Dumplings:
225 g (8 oz) self-raising flour
100 g (4 oz) shredded suet
a pinch of salt
5 ml (1 tsp) caraway seeds

1. Soak the meat in cold water overnight. Drain it and place in a large saucepan, pour over enough water to cover and add the cloves and peppercorns. Bring to the boil, skim, reduce the heat and simmer, covered, for 25 minutes per 500 g (1 lb) plus 25 minutes. Add the carrots and the onions about 1 hour before the end of the cooking time.
2. To make the dumplings: sift the flour into a mixing bowl. Stir in the suet, salt and caraway seeds, with enough cold water to make a firm dough. Shape the dough into 16 small balls and drop them into the cooking liquid 20 minutes before the end, re-covering the pan immediately you have added the dumplings.
3. When the beef is cooked, lift it out and place on a serving dish. Drain the vegetables and dumplings with a perforated spoon and place them around the meat. Keep warm.
4. Measure 550 ml (1 pint) of the cooking liquid and place in a sauce-pan. Mix the Bisto Powder with a little cold water and stir in. Bring to the boil, stirring; pour into a warmed gravy boat and serve with the meat.

SAUERBRATEN

Serves 4

1 large onion, sliced in rings
125 ml (¼ pint) dry red wine
125 ml (¼ pint) red wine vinegar
250 ml (½ pint) cold water
6 whole black peppercorns
a bay leaf
a blade of mace

1.4 kg (3 lb) joint of topside of beef
30 ml (2 tbsp) oil
1 leek, trimmed and sliced
1 large carrot, peeled and diced
1 stick of celery, chopped in small dice
30 ml (2 tbsp) Bisto Powder
50 g (2 oz) seedless raisins

1. Place the onion, wine, vinegar, water, peppercorns, bay leaf and mace in a saucepan. Bring to the boil and simmer for 1 minute; then remove from the heat and allow to cool.

Sauerbraten; Boiled Beef and Carrots

2. Wipe the beef with kitchen paper and place it in a deep bowl. Pour over the red wine mixture and turn the beef in the marinade. Cover the bowl and leave in a cool place for 48 hours, turning the beef over occasionally.

3. Remove the beef and dry with kitchen paper. Preheat the oven to 180°C/350°F/Gas Mark 4.

4. Heat the oil in a large, flameproof casserole and brown the beef on all sides. Remove to a plate and add the leek, carrot and celery to the casserole. Fry over a low heat until lightly browned. Strain excess fat.

5. Strain the marinade and add three-quarters of it to the casserole. Blend the Bisto Powder with the remaining marinade until smooth and stir it into the casserole. Bring to the boil, stirring constantly; replace the beef.

6. Cover the casserole and cook it in the oven for about 1¾ hours or until the beef is tender. Add the raisins and cook for 10 more minutes.

7. Serve carved into 5 mm (¼-inch) slices and spoon over a little of the sauce. Serve the rest of the sauce separately.

BEEF ROLY-POLY

Serves 4

30 ml (2 tbsp) oil
1 onion, chopped
350 g (12 oz) lean minced beef
15 ml (1 tbsp) Bisto Powder
15 ml (1 tbsp) plain flour
400 g (14 oz) can of plum tomatoes
30 ml (2 tbsp) tomato purée

Suet-crust pastry:
175 g (6 oz) self-raising flour
2.5 ml (½ tsp) salt
75 g (3 oz) shredded beef or vegetable suet
about 90 ml (6 tbsp) cold water
30 ml (2 tbsp) creamed horseradish
To glaze:
beaten egg or milk

1. Heat the oil in a pan and fry the onion and minced beef until the onion is soft and the beef lightly browned, about 5 minutes. Add the Bisto Powder and plain flour, and fry, stirring occasionally, for 1 minute. Add the tomatoes and their juice, and the tomato purée. Bring to the boil, stirring; lower the heat and simmer for 30 minutes, stirring frequently. Allow to cool.

2. To make the suet-crust pastry: sift the self-raising flour and salt into a bowl and stir in the suet. Add the cold water and mix to a soft dough with a round-bladed knife. Knead lightly on a floured surface; then chill for 30 minutes before using.

3. Preheat the oven to 200°C/400°F/Gas Mark 6. Roll out the pastry on a

Beef Roly-Poly

lightly floured surface to a square measuring roughly 30 cm (12 inches).
Spread the creamed horseradish and the mince mixture on the pastry.
4. Roll the pastry up and lift the roll on to a lightly greased baking sheet.
Score the top with a knife and brush it with beaten egg or milk to glaze.
5. Bake for about 45 minutes until golden; cover the top with foil if the
roly-poly starts to over-brown.
6. Serve cut in thick slices with Bisto gravy and vegetables.

VEAL

Veal is young, immature beef and although veal escalopes are a familiar sight in the majority of restaurants, veal cuts are not widely seen in butchers' shop windows outside large towns. It is a fairly dry meat, with little fat; this means that it needs careful cooking if it is not to taste bland, and it is often served with sauces and stuffings to counteract this.

Choosing and buying veal

Look for soft, finely-grained, moist meat that is very pale pink in colour; avoid any that looks dry and brown. Any fat should be firm and very white. Bones should be soft and almost translucent. Any gelatinous tissue around the meat is quite normal; it simply indicates a young animal and will shrink and soften during cooking.

Cuts of veal

Fillet (thick flank)

The most expensive cut, from which *escalopes* and *cutlets* are cut. The fillet can be roasted in the piece; due to its prohibitive cost, however, it is more usual to buy thin slices and have them beaten out as escalopes.

Loin

A little cheaper than fillet but still expensive. The *best end*, which contains the kidney, is considered a prime roasting joint. *Chops* are cut from the *chump end*.

Shoulder

Can be braised or roasted. Usually sold boned so it can be stuffed for roasting.

Breast

Excellent for stewing or braising. Can be roasted if boned and rolled.

Knuckle (shin)

Suitable for long, slow cooking in stews and casseroles.

Middle neck

An economical cut, with a high proportion of bone. Usually sold in *cutlets* for braising or boned as *pie veal*.

Calves' feet

Highly gelatinous; used for making meat jellies.

Carving veal

Shoulder and breast joints are normally boned before purchase and tied into shape, making them easy to carve into slices.

Loin on the bone is carved in the same way as loin of pork.

VEAL, ASPARAGUS AND MUSHROOM PIE

Serves 4–6

Phyllo pastry, a paper-thin, crispy crust, is used in local forms all over the world. In Austria it is the wrapping for apple strudel, in Egypt it has cream and dried fruits poured over it to make a calorie-laden pudding called Om Ali and in China it makes the famous Spring Rolls. In this pie, the pastry encloses layers of veal, asparagus and mushrooms in a creamy sauce. Most large supermarkets have the pastry in their freezer cabinets or look for it in delicatessens or shops selling Greek food.

60 ml (4 tbsp) oil
1 onion, sliced
500 g (1 lb) pie veal, minced
225 g (8 oz) mushrooms, chopped
15 ml (1 tbsp) Bisto Powder
125 ml (¼ pt) cold water
125 g (5 oz) carton of fromage frais

225 g (8 oz) cooked ham, chopped
2.5 ml (½ tsp) paprika
225 g (8 oz) phyllo pastry, thawed
oil or melted butter
225 g (8 oz) asparagus spears, cooked
and trimmed

1. Heat the oil in a frying-pan and fry the onion until soft. Stir in the veal and fry for 4–5 minutes until the meat is lightly coloured. Add the mushrooms and cook for 1 minute.

2. Blend the Bisto Powder and the water, add to the pan, bring to the boil, stirring, lower the heat and simmer for 5 minutes. Remove from the heat and stir in the fromage frais, ham and paprika. Return to the heat for 1 minute; allow to bubble for 10 minutes until excess moisture has evaporated.

3. Unroll the pastry and divide the sheets in half, cutting from the centre of one long side to the other. Keep the sheets covered with a damp tea towel or they will quickly dry out and crack when you try to work with them.

4. Lightly brush a shallow ovenproof dish measuring roughly 20×30 cm (8×12 inches) with oil or melted butter and line it with half the phyllo pastry sheets, brushing each sheet with oil or melted butter before adding the next. Spoon in the veal mixture and top with the asparagus spears.

5. Brush the pastry edges with oil or melted butter and cover the pie with the remaining pastry sheets, again brushing each one with oil or butter. (If you have not used all the sheets in the packet the remainder can be refrozen.)

6. Tuck the pastry into the sides of the pie. Brush the top with oil or melted butter and score a diamond pattern with a sharp knife.

7. Preheat the oven to 190°C/375°F/Gas Mark 5. Bake the pie for 45 minutes or until it is a rich, golden brown. Serve with a mixed salad.

VEAL PARMIGIANA

Serves 4 ✱

You will find cartons of crushed or puréed tomatoes in most large supermarkets these days, and they make light work of preparing pizza toppings, spaghetti sauces or, as in this recipe, a rich tomato sauce for veal escalopes. I am in favour of anything that saves me time when I'm cooking, without any sacrifice of flavour, and so I always keep a couple of these cartons of crushed tomatoes in my store cupboard.

4 veal escalopes
60 ml (4 tbsp) plain flour
1 egg, beaten
45 ml (3 tbsp) dried brown or white
   breadcrumbs
30 ml (2 tbsp) grated parmesan cheese
oil for frying
25 g (1 oz) butter
4 slices of Parma ham

Sauce:
250 ml (½ pint) crushed or puréed
   tomatoes
15 ml (1 tbsp) Bisto Powder
5 ml (1 tsp) granulated sugar
5 ml (1 tsp) dried basil
Topping:
75 g (3 oz) Mozzarella cheese, sliced

1. Coat the veal escalopes in the flour and brush with beaten egg. Mix together the breadcrumbs and parmesan and press over the escalopes. Set aside.
2. Heat about 5 mm (¼ inch) oil in a frying-pan and add the butter; when hot, fry the escalopes for 3–4 minutes or until cooked, turning once. Drain and place in a shallow ovenproof dish.
3. Preheat the oven to 180°C/350°F/Gas Mark 4. Fold the slices of Parma ham in half and tuck in between the escalopes in the dish.
4. To make the sauce: place the tomatoes in a pan. Add the Bisto Powder, sugar and basil and bring to the boil, stirring. Simmer for 1 minute and then pour the sauce over the escalopes. Arrange the Mozzarella slices over the dish.
5. Bake for 10–15 minutes until the Mozzarella has melted. Brown quickly under a hot grill if you like. Serve at once with sauté or fried potatoes and a green vegetable or salad.

Veal, Asparagus and Mushroom Pie; Veal Parmigiana

VEAL MARSALA

Serves 6

4 veal escalopes, beaten out until thin
30 ml (2 tbsp) plain flour
1 size 3 egg, beaten
50 g (2 oz) dried breadcrumbs
15 ml (1 tbsp) grated parmesan cheese
45 ml (3 tbsp) oil
25 g (1 oz) butter
1 onion, chopped finely

175 g (6 oz) tiny whole button
  mushrooms
250 ml (½ pint) gravy made with Bisto
  Rich Gravy Granules for Chicken
75 ml (3 fl oz) Marsala
60 ml (4 tbsp) double cream
To garnish:
30 ml (2 tbsp) chopped fresh parsley

1. Beat the veal escalopes between two sheets of cling film or waxed paper, with a steak hammer or rolling-pin, until they are very thin. Halve them across the centre. Coat with the flour, beaten egg, and mixed breadcrumbs and parmesan.
2. Heat the oil and butter in a frying-pan and fry the escalopes for 2 minutes on each side or until golden brown. Remove to a serving platter and keep warm.
3. Add the onion and mushrooms to the pan and fry until the onion is soft. Stir in the gravy and Marsala and bring to the boil. Allow to bubble for 1 minute and then stir in the cream.
4. Spoon the sauce over the veal and serve garnished with the chopped parsley. Accompany with sauté or new potatoes and grilled tomatoes.

VEAL CHOPS BONNE FEMME

Serves 4   ✱

4 × 2 cm (¾ inch) veal chops
60 ml (4 tbsp) oil
50 g (2 oz) butter
12 baby onions, peeled and left whole
6 rashers of streaky bacon, rind and
  bones removed, cut into 2.5 cm
  (1 inch) pieces

8 small carrots, peeled
12 small new potatoes
100 g (4 oz) button mushrooms
30 ml (2 tbsp) Bisto Powder
400 ml (¾ pint) cold water
125 ml (¼ pint) dry white wine
a bay leaf
5 ml (1 tsp) dried mixed herbs

1. Trim the chops. Heat the oil and butter in a large frying-pan and lightly brown the chops over a brisk heat on both sides. Place in a casserole.
2. Add the onions and bacon to the pan and fry for 2 minutes. Add the carrots and potatoes and fry until the bacon is transparent and the vegetables start to brown. Add to the casserole, with the mushrooms.

Veal Chops Bonne Femme; Veal Marsala

3. Preheat the oven to 180°C/350°F/Gas Mark 4. Blend the Bisto Powder with a little of the water. Pour the wine into the pan and bubble for 30 seconds. Add the rest of the water and the Bisto mixture and bring to the boil, stirring. Add to the casserole, with the herbs.

4. Cook, covered, for 45 minutes or until the veal is cooked and the vegetables are tender. Remove the bay leaf before serving.

LAMB

Most lambs are slaughtered when they are between three and twelve months old and the distinctive, delicate flavour of their meat has made lamb a great favourite with the British public. Home-produced lamb is available between March and November, although it is most plentiful between August and November. Imported lamb from Australia and New Zealand fills the gap during the winter months.

Choosing and buying lamb

A lamb joint should have thick, lean meat covering the bone and a moderate layer of fat, covered with a soft, pliable skin. Leg and shoulder joints should have a plump appearance. The flesh should be fine-grained and pinkish in colour, with firm white fat. Dark red flesh and yellow fat indicate a lamb that is too old.

Cuts of lamb

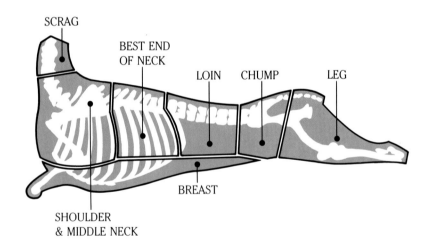

Scrag and middle neck

Usually sold as *chops* for stewing or braising. Traditionally used for Irish stew and Lancashire hot-pot.

Saddle of lamb

A large roasting joint consisting of the whole loin from both sides of the animal in one piece.

Shoulder

A tender, roasting joint. Sold on the bone or boned for stuffing and rolling. More fatty than leg, it has an excellent flavour and can be purchased either whole or cut into *blade* and *knuckle*, both of which can be roasted or braised.

Best end of neck

Can be purchased as a roasting joint with a row of about 7 rib bones. Ask the butcher to saw through the vertebrae, or 'chine' bone, without removing it from the joint, to make carving easier. It can be roasted on the bone, or boned, stuffed and rolled. The joint is also sold divided into *cutlets*, each with one rib bone, for grilling or frying. Two best ends of neck joined together and curved, bones outwards, make a *crown roast*. The centre of the roast is filled with a savoury stuffing. If the two best ends of neck face each other, with the fat side outwards, they are called a *guard of honour*. These are both special occasion roasts.

Loin

This can either be roasted in the piece or boned, stuffed and rolled. It is usually divided into *loin end* and *chump end* and cut into chops for grilling or frying. Chump chops are recognisable by the small, round bone in the centre. *'Barnsley'* or *'butterfly'* *chops* are double loin chops.

Leg

Excellent for roasting on the bone, or boned, stuffed and rolled. The leg can be divided into the *fillet (top) end* and *shank end*.

Breast

A long, thin cut, streaked with fat and lean. When boned, rolled and stuffed, it is a very economical cut for roasting and braising.

New cuts

Designed to supplement rather than replace the traditional cuts, these are boneless lean joints, roasts and steaks that can be cut to any size to suit the customer. One of the best is the 'valentine steak' cut from a thick loin chop which is cut almost completely in half and opened out to a heart shape.

ROAST LAMB

Lamb makes a marvellous Sunday roast for the family, whether it's home-produced spring lamb or imported from New Zealand. Choose your joint depending on how many people you have to feed; a large joint such as a leg will provide enough for a family of six to eight whereas for two or three a rack of best end of neck cutlets will be just right.

Allow about 350 g (12 oz) of lamb on the bone per person and about 175 g (6 oz) per person if the joint has been boned. The most suitable cuts for roasting are leg, shoulder, loin, rack or saddle. Boned joints can be rolled, tied and roasted just as they are or spread with a savoury herb or nut stuffing before rolling.

Trim the joint of any excess fat if you like, and then weigh it to calculate the cooking time, allowing 20 to 25 minutes per 500 g (1 lb) plus 20 to 25 minutes depending on how well done you like your lamb. If you like your meat really pink, allow 15 minutes per 500 g (1 lb) plus 15 minutes and then check it; if you prefer it cooked through, allow the longer time. Roast at 220°C/425°F/Gas Mark 7 for the first 10 minutes and then reduce the oven to 190°C/375°F/Gas Mark 5 for the remaining cooking time.

Rosemary goes very well with lamb. If you have a boned joint, tuck a few sprigs of fresh rosemary into the centre of the roll. For a joint on the bone, make slits all over the outer skin with a sharp knife and tuck small sprigs of rosemary into them. Garlic is also good with lamb: tuck a couple of cloves inside or push slivers into slits in the skin.

Carving lamb

Leg: with the meatier side uppermost, carve a narrow, wedge-shaped piece of meat from the middle, right down to the bone. Carve slices from each side. Remove any excess fat from the underside and slice along the length.

Shoulder: hold the joint at the shank end, skin uppermost. Cut a wedge-shaped slice through the middle in the angle between the shoulder blade and the foreleg bone. Carve slices from each side until the shoulder blade and foreleg bones are reached. Turn the joint over and carve slices along the length.

Traditional accompaniments for roast lamb are roast potatoes, peas, redcurrant or mint jelly and a rich gravy made with Bisto Powder blended with the meat juices in the tin. Mint sauce also goes well, but if you are serving wine the acidity of mint sauce could spoil it.

Roast Lamb

LAMB HUSSAR

Serves 4 ★ *Without the soured cream*

Middle neck of lamb joints make an excellent and economic casserole. This one-pot meal freezes well, but do not add the soured cream until you have defrosted it ready for eating. You can also make this the day before it is needed, keep it in the refrigerator overnight and then reheat it and add the soured cream the following day.

1 kg (2 lb) middle neck of lamb
30 ml (2 tbsp) plain flour
5 ml (1 tsp) paprika
about 30 ml (2 tbsp) oil
25 g (1 oz) butter
8 button onions or shallots, peeled
225 g (8 oz) baby carrots, peeled
400 g (14 oz) can of chopped tomatoes
15 ml (1 tbsp) Bisto Powder

250 ml (½ pint) cold water
500 g (1 lb) potatoes, peeled and cut
 into small chunks
To finish:
125 ml (¼ pint) fresh soured cream
15 ml (1 tbsp) cornflour
15 ml (1 tbsp) chopped fresh parsley

1. Divide the meat into joints. Mix together the flour and paprika and coat the lamb.
2. Heat the oil and butter in a frying-pan and quickly brown the lamb on both sides. Lift it out with a draining spoon and transfer to a large casserole.
3. Add a little more oil to the pan if necessary and fry the onions and carrots until lightly browned. Transfer to the casserole.
4. Add any flour left on the plate to the pan, pour in the tomatoes and add the Bisto Powder and cold water. Bring to the boil, stirring, lower heat and simmer uncovered for 5 minutes; remove from the heat.
5. Preheat the oven to 180°C/350°F/Gas Mark 4.
6. Add the potatoes to the casserole and pour in the tomato mixture from the frying-pan. Cover the casserole and cook in the oven for 1½ hours, or until lamb is tender.
7. Lift the meat and vegetables from the sauce and place them in a serving dish. Keep warm. Skim any fat from the surface of the sauce. Beat together the soured cream and cornflour until smooth. Place the casserole on the heat if flameproof, or transfer the sauce to a frying-pan and set over the heat. Stir in the soured cream and bring the sauce back to the boil, stirring constantly. Simmer for 1 minute and then pour over the lamb and vegetables and serve sprinkled with the chopped parsley.

GREEK MEAT LOAF

Serves 4

This meat loaf is slightly unusual in that it combines layers of minced lamb with aubergine; it's a bit like a Moussaka without a creamy topping. Serve the loaf cut into thick slices with a tomato sauce spiked with little chilli powder or a pinch of your favourite herb.

2 large aubergines, sliced
30 ml (2 tbsp)oil
1 large onion, chopped
1 green pepper, de-seeded and
  chopped
175 g (6 oz) mushrooms, sliced
2 cloves of garlic, crushed

500 g (1 lb) lean minced lamb
2 tomatoes, peeled and chopped
15 ml (1 tbsp) Bisto Powder
250 ml (½ pint) tomato juice
5 ml (1 tsp) dried thyme
2 size 3 eggs, beaten

1. Spread out the aubergine slices on a plate, sprinkle with salt, cover and leave for 30 minutes. Drain and rinse. Blanch the slices in boiling, salted water for 1 minute and then drain and set aside.
2. Heat the oil in a deep frying-pan and fry the onion, pepper, mushrooms and garlic until the onion is soft. Stir in the minced lamb, breaking up any lumps with a wooden spoon, and cook for 3–4 minutes until the meat becomes pale and starts to brown. Spoon off any excess fat.
3. Add the tomatoes, Bisto Powder, tomato juice and thyme and bring to the boil. Simmer for about 5 minutes, and then remove from the heat and leave to cool a little.
4. Stir the beaten eggs into the meat mixture.
5. Preheat the oven to 180°C/350°F/Gas Mark 4. Brush a 1 kg (2 lb) loaf tin with oil and line the base with greaseproof paper. Arrange a layer of overlapping aubergine slices over the bottom and sides of the tin. Spoon in half the meat mixture and then put in another layer of aubergine. Finish with the remaining meat and the rest of the aubergine slices.
6. Cover the tin with oiled foil, place on a baking sheet and cook in the oven for 45 minutes. Leave to stand for 2 minutes and then carefully run a knife around the inside edge of the tin and turn the loaf out on to a serving plate.
7. Serve with boiled rice and tomato sauce.

Greek Meat Loaf

LAMB HOTPOT

Serves 4

45 ml (3 tbsp) oil
1 kg (2 lb) middle neck lamb chops,
   trimmed of excess fat
3 onions, sliced thinly into rings
250 ml (½ pint) gravy, made with Bisto
   Rich Gravy Granules as directed

100 g (4 oz) button mushrooms,
   quartered
100 g (4 oz) black pudding, skinned
   and sliced
1 kg (2 lb) celeriac, peeled and sliced
   5 mm (¼ inch) thick
25 g (1 oz) melted butter

1. Preheat the oven to 180°C/350°F/Gas Mark 4. Heat the oil in a frying-pan and quickly brown the chops on both sides. Place in a casserole.
2. Soften the onions in the pan; do not brown. Pour in the gravy and add the mushrooms. Bring to the boil and pour over the chops. Cover with the sliced black pudding and then the celeriac. Cook, covered, for 2 hours.
3. Brush the melted butter over the celeriac slices and cook for 20 to 25 minutes or until the celeriac is brown with crisp edges.

STUFFED BREAST OF LAMB

Serves 6 to 8

2 breasts of lamb, weighing about 1 kg
   (2 lb), trimmed and boned
Stuffing:
225 g (8 oz) peeled chestnuts
30 ml (2 tbsp) oil
1 onion, chopped

100 g (4 oz) streaky bacon, rind and
   bones removed, and chopped
15 ml (1 tbsp) chopped fresh thyme or
   5 ml (1 tsp) dried thyme
15 ml (1 tbsp) chopped fresh parsley
15 ml (1 tbsp) Bisto Powder
30 ml (2 tbsp) milk

1. Lay the breasts of lamb on a board, skin-side down, so they overlap a little. Preheat the oven to 170°C/325°F/Gas Mark 3.
2. Grind the chestnuts finely in a food processor or nut mill.
3. Heat the oil in a pan and fry the onion and bacon until soft. Remove from the heat and stir in the chestnuts, thyme, parsley, Bisto Powder and milk. Turn into a bowl and allow to cool.
4. Spread the stuffing over the lamb breasts almost to the edge; then roll up and tie the roll at 2.5 cm (1-inch) intervals with thin string.
5. Place the meat in a roasting tin and cover with foil. Cook in the oven for 2 hours, basting occasionally with the pan juices.
6. Set the meat aside, covered, for 10 minutes; then carve into thick slices. Serve with roast potatoes, vegetables and Bisto Gravy.

Lamb Hotpot; Stuffed Breast of Lamb

LAMB MEATBALLS IN RICH CHEESE AND ONION SAUCE

Serves 4

Meatballs:
500 g (1 lb) lean minced lamb
1 onion, chopped finely
5 ml (1 tsp) chopped fresh ginger
2.5 ml (½ tsp) ground cardamom
2.5 ml (½ tsp) ground cinnamon
15 ml (1 tbsp) finely chopped fresh
  mint
60 ml (4 tbsp) mincemeat
1 size 3 egg, beaten

15 ml (1 tbsp) Bisto Powder
30 ml (2 tbsp) plain flour
oil for shallow-frying
Sauce:
400 ml (¾ pint) onion sauce, made
  with Bisto Onion Sauce Granules as
  directed
75 g (3 oz) Cheddar cheese, grated
15 ml (1 tbsp) grated parmesan cheese
5 ml (1 tsp) made English mustard

1. To make the meatballs: place the lamb in a large bowl and mix in the onion, ginger, cardamom, cinnamon, mint and mincemeat until well combined. Stir in the beaten egg to bind the mixture.
2. Shape the mixture into 16 small balls. Mix together the Bisto Powder and flour and roll the meatballs in this until coated.
3. Heat 5 mm (¼ inch) of oil in a frying-pan and fry the meatballs over a low heat for 12–15 minutes, shaking the pan occasionally, until they are browned on all sides. Remove with a draining spoon and place in a single layer in a shallow ovenproof dish.
4. Preheat the oven to 180°C/350°F/Gas Mark 4. To make the sauce: first make up the onion sauce and then stir the Cheddar, parmesan and mustard into the hot sauce. Pour the sauce over the meatballs.
5. Bake the meatballs in the oven for 10–15 minutes, or until hot.

LAMB CHOP TOAD-IN-THE-HOLE

Serves 2

4 lamb cutlets
50 g (2 oz) lard or dripping
Batter:
100 g (4 oz) plain flour
15 ml (1 tbsp) Bisto Powder

a pinch of salt
1 size 1 egg
125 ml (¼ pint) milk
125 ml (¼ pint) cold water

1. Trim the cutlets of excess fat and place them in a roasting tin. Cut the lard or dripping into small pieces and dot over the cutlets.
2. To make the batter: sift the flour, Bisto Powder and salt together. Make

Lamb Meatballs in Rich Cheese and Onion Sauce; Lamb Chop Toad-in-the-hole

a well in the centre and break in the egg. Add half the milk and half the water and gradually mix. Beat until smooth; add the rest of the liquid and beat or whisk for about 5 minutes to incorporate plenty of air into the batter. Leave to stand for 1 hour.

3. Preheat the oven to 220°C/425°F/Gas Mark 7. Place the tin of lamb cutlets in the oven and roast for 10 minutes; turn the chops once.

4. Pour the batter into the tin and bake for 40–45 minutes, until the batter is well risen and golden brown.

LAMB DHAL

Serves 6

A dhal is a popular dish in India; the name indicates that the sauce has been thickened with lentils. I usually try and buy 'continental' (or brown) lentils, because they do not disintegrate during cooking and so the final texture of the dish is better.

45 ml (3 tbsp) oil
1 kg (2 lb) lean lamb leg or shoulder, trimmed of excess fat and cut into 2.5 cm (1-inch) cubes
2 onions, sliced thinly
2 celery sticks, chopped
2 cloves of garlic, crushed
15 ml (1 tbsp) ground coriander
5 ml (1 tsp) ground cumin
5 ml (1 tsp) ground turmeric

5 ml (1 tsp) chilli powder
2.5 ml (½ tsp) ground ginger
2.5 ml (½ tsp) ground cinnamon
500 ml (1 pint) gravy, made with Bisto Rich Gravy Granules as directed
198 g (7 oz) can of plum tomatoes
225 g (8 oz) continental lentils
To finish:
150 g (5 oz) natural yogurt

1. Heat the oil in a large, flameproof casserole or saucepan and fry the lamb in 4 or 5 batches for 2–3 minutes until the meat is no longer pink; stir frequently to prevent sticking. Remove each batch with a draining spoon and set aside.

2. Add the onions, celery and garlic to the casserole, with a little more oil if necessary, and cook over a gentle heat until softened, stirring occasionally.

3. Sprinkle in the coriander, cumin, turmeric, chilli, ginger and cinnamon and stir to coat the onion mixture. Fry over a gentle heat for 1 minute. Return the meat to the pan with any juice that has run out of it and pour in the gravy and tomatoes and their juice. Stir in the lentils.

4. Bring to boiling point, lower the heat, cover the pan and simmer gently for about 1¾ hours, or until the lamb is tender.

5. Serve topped with yogurt and accompanied by boiled rice or potatoes.

Lamb Dhal

PORK

Pork

Pork used not to be sold in summer (when there was no 'R' in the month) because it goes off very quickly. With refrigeration, however, it is widely available all year round. Pork still needs to be bought as fresh as possible, and must only ever be eaten well cooked.

Choosing and buying pork

Pork flesh should be pale pink, firm textured and smooth, with firm, milky-white fat. The skin, or rind, should be thin, pliable, smooth and free of hairs. Ask the butcher to score the rind with deep, close cuts, so that the heat penetrates the meat and the rind crackles during roasting.

Cuts of pork

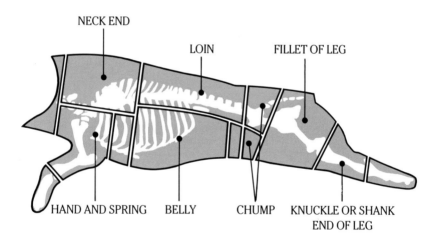

NECK END

LOIN

FILLET OF LEG

HAND AND SPRING   BELLY   CHUMP   KNUCKLE OR SHANK END OF LEG

Neck end
(spare rib and blade bone)

A large, economical roasting joint that is excellent when boned, stuffed and rolled. Can be divided into blade and spare rib, both of which can be roasted, braised or stewed. Spare rib chops can be grilled, braised or fried; they should not be confused with Chinese spare ribs, which are the rib bones from the boned belly.

Trotters

The feet are usually salted and boiled or used for making brawn.

Loin

Can be roasted on the bone, or boned, stuffed and rolled. Can be divided into loin chops (with or without the kidney) and chump chops, which are large and meaty. Both can be grilled, fried or roasted. Good for producing crackling.

Hand and spring

A large joint for roasting, often divided into hand and shank. Both hand and shank can also be casseroled or stewed.

Belly

A long, thin cut with streaks of fat and lean. The stuffed thick end makes a cheap roast. Belly pork slices are better grilled or fried than casseroled, as they are quite fatty.

Leg

Can be cut into four or more roasting joints, or divided into the fillet (top) end and knuckle end. The fillet is the better roasting joint and it can be boned and stuffed. It is also sold sliced into steaks for grilling and frying. Knuckle end is ideal for boning and stuffing.

Tenderloin

A lean, tender cut, from underneath the backbone of the loin. It is sometimes called pork fillet but should not be confused with the fillet end of the leg. Can be stuffed and rolled for roasting, or sliced or cubed for stir-frying or coating with a sauce.

New cuts

Look out for some of the new, boneless range of cuts designed for today's busy shopper. They come from a complete side of pork, which is boned and then divided into joints which are easy to carve and serve, plus steaks which are trimmed of fat and intended for quick cooking by grilling and frying.

ORIENTAL SPARE RIBS

Serves 4

1 kg (2 lb) Chinese pork spare ribs	*50 g (2 oz) demerara sugar*
30 ml (2 tbsp) oil	*15 ml (1 tbsp) tomato purée*
1 large onion, chopped finely	*5 ml (1 tsp) paprika*
15 ml (1 tbsp) Bisto Powder	*15 ml (1 tbsp) Worcestershire sauce*
125 ml (¼ pint) unsweetened	*30 ml (2 tbsp) malt vinegar*
* pineapple juice*	*salt*
125 ml(¼ pint) cold water	

1. Preheat the oven to 200°C/400°F/Gas Mark 6. Place the ribs skin side up in a roasting tin. Sprinkle with salt and roast for 30 minutes.

2. Heat the oil in a pan and fry the onion until soft. Sprinkle in the Bisto Powder and then remove from the heat and blend in the pineapple juice, cold water, sugar, tomato purée, paprika, Worcestershire sauce and vinegar. Bring to the boil, stirring; then set aside.

3. Pour off the fat from the roasting tin and pour the sauce over the ribs. Cook for a further 1 hour, basting frequently with the sauce. Accompany with sweetcorn and boiled rice if serving as a main course.

ROAST PORK WITH CRACKLING

Pork is an excellent buy all year round. There are prime cuts and inexpensive joints to choose from and they all roast well and have a rich flavour. Allow about 350 g (12 oz) of meat per person if the joint has a bone, and 175 g (6 oz) per person if it hasn't.

Pork must always be eaten well done, so allow 30 minutes per 500 g (1 lb) plus 30 minutes, at 190°C/375°F/Gas Mark 5. Accompany with roast or boiled potatoes, vegetables, sage and onion stuffing (if liked) and Bisto gravy. Apple or gooseberry sauce provides a sharp taste to contrast with the rich pork meat; try stirring 5 ml (1 tsp) of sage into the sauce, for an extra tang.

To achieve proper crackling you really need to buy a joint of fresh pork; I find frozen joints never seem to crackle properly, even though the meat is as good as fresh. Ask the butcher to score the skin for you. Brush the skin with oil and rub it heavily with salt. Roast in the usual way but avoid basting the skin with the pan juices during cooking, because this will impede the crackling process. If the crackling still looks a bit chewy when the joint is ready, cut it away from the meat in one piece and place it under a hot grill for a few minutes.

A French friend of mine gave me this tip: spread the scored skin thickly with mayonnaise and sprinkle over coarse sea salt before roasting. She said it was an infallible way of achieving perfect crackling every time and I must say that on the times I have tried it the crackling was indeed perfect.

Carving pork
Leg (shank end): Remove some of the crackling to make carving easier. Cut thin slices down to, and around the bone, as far as possible. When the shank bone is reached, carve at an angle over the top of the bone. Turn the joint over and cut slanting slices down towards the thin end of the bone.
Leg (fillet end): Carve slices through to the bone on either side of it.
Loin: Remove the chine bone. Cut through the fat just under the crackling and remove part or all of the crackling, before carving in thin slices down to the bones. Serve the crackling broken into strips.

Roast Pork with Crackling

RED PEPPER MEATBALLS

Serves 4–6

✳

Red pepper sauce:
2 red peppers, de-seeded and chopped
1 onion, chopped
250 ml (½ pint) gravy, made with
*   15 ml (1 tbsp) Bisto Rich Gravy*
*   Granules and 250 ml (½ pint)*
*   boiling water*
250 ml (½ pint) tomato juice
5 ml (1 tsp) dried basil
5 ml (1 tsp) caster sugar
a dash of Tabasco sauce
Meat balls:
350 g (12 oz) lean pork, minced

225 g (8 oz) unsmoked gammon,
*   minced*
5 ml (1 tsp) dried sage
5 ml (1 tsp) Dijon mustard
4 spring onions, trimmed and chopped
*   finely*
50 g (2 oz) fresh wholemeal
*   breadcrumbs*
15 ml (1 tbsp) Bisto Powder
2 size 3 eggs, beaten
50 g (2 oz) plain flour
60 ml (4 tbsp) oil

1. To make the red pepper sauce: place all ingredients in a large saucepan and bring to the boil. Lower the heat and simmer gently, covered, for 1 hour. Liquidise. Return to the saucepan and set aside.

2. To make the meatballs: place the pork, gammon, sage, mustard, spring onions, breadcrumbs and Bisto powder in a mixing bowl and mix well. Stir in the eggs. Shape with your hands into 24 small, even-sized balls and roll in the flour.

3. Preheat the oven to 180°C/350°F/Gas Mark 4. Heat the oil in a frying pan and brown the meatballs over a brisk heat for 4–5 minutes, shaking the pan at regular intervals. Transfer to a casserole.

4. Bring the sauce back to simmering point and pour it over the meatballs. Cook, covered, for 35–40 minutes. Serve with boiled rice, pasta or mashed potatoes.

Red Pepper Meatballs; Oriental Spare Ribs (page 47)

PORK FILLET EN CROÛTE

Serves 6

2 large tenderloins
Stuffing:
25 g (1 oz) butter
1 onion, chopped
1 clove of garlic, crushed
175 g (6 oz) field mushrooms,
*   chopped finely*
15 ml (1 tbsp) chopped fresh parsley

50 g (2 oz) fresh wholemeal
*   breadcrumbs*
15 ml (1 tbsp) Bisto Powder
60 ml (4 tbsp) oil
Wrapping:
6 thin slices of cooked ham
500 g (1 lb) puff pastry
To glaze:
beaten egg

1. With a small, sharp knife, remove any skin and fat from the meat. Split each tenderloin lengthways down the centre, without cutting it completely in half, and open out. Place the meat between two sheets of cling film and beat with a rolling pin until thin.

2. To make the stuffing: melt the butter and fry the onion and garlic until soft but not browned. Stir in the mushrooms and cook until soft. Turn up the heat a little and allow the moisture from the mushrooms to evaporate. When the mixture is quite dry, remove from the heat and stir in the parsley, breadcrumbs and Bisto Powder. Allow to cool.

3. Spoon the stuffing down the centre of 1 tenderloin. Top with the remaining tenderloin so the stuffing is completely enclosed. Tie the meat at 2.5 cm (1-inch) intervals with thin string.

4. Preheat the oven to 180°C/350°F/Gas Mark 4. Heat the oil in a roasting tin placed on the hob of the stove and brown the meat quickly on all sides. Transfer to the oven and cook, basting from time to time, for 45 minutes. Remove from the oven and allow meat to go completely cold.

5. Remove the string. Wrap the slices of ham around the meat roll.

6. On a lightly floured surface, roll out the pastry about 5 mm (¼ inch) thick, to a rectangle large enough to enclose the meat. Place the pork in the centre of the pastry and fold the pastry round it, brushing with water to seal the joins. Decorate with any pastry trimmings, fixing them in place by brushing with water.

7. Chill for 30 minutes. Preheat the oven to 220°C/425°F/Gas Mark 7.

8. Brush the pastry with the beaten egg and bake for 30–35 minutes until golden brown.

Pork Fillet en Croûte

PORK AND CRANBERRY PIE

Serves 8

Filling:
*500 g (1 lb) lean pork, such as
    shoulder steaks, minced*
2 onions, chopped finely
5 ml (1 tsp) dried sage
1.25 ml (¼ tsp) ground mace
350 g (12 oz) pork sausage meat
15 ml (1 tbsp) Bisto Powder
*225 g (8 oz) frozen chopped spinach,
    thawed*
Pastry:
350 g (12 oz) plain flour

2.5 ml (½ tsp) salt
125 ml (¼ pint) mixed milk and water
100 g (4 oz) lard or white vegetable fat
milk to glaze
Topping:
225 g (8 oz) cranberries
75 g (3 oz) granulated sugar
*60 ml (4 tbsp) cranberry or redcurrant
    jelly*
15 ml (1 tbsp) lemon juice

1. To make the filling: mix the pork, onions, sage, mace, sausage meat and Bisto Powder together in a large bowl. Place the spinach in a frying-pan and heat it gently so that any moisture runs out and evaporates. When the spinach is dry, remove from the pan and squeeze between two dinner plates to remove any remaining moisture. Allow the spinach to cool and then stir into the meat mixture.

2. To make the pastry: sift the flour and salt into a bowl. Heat the milk and water with the lard or vegetable fat until boiling; then stir into the flour and mix well. Knead when cool enough to handle and use warm.

3. Roll out the pastry on a lightly floured surface and line a greased 20 cm (8-inch) loose-bottomed round tin. Chill for 30 minutes. Place a few pieces of crumpled foil in the pastry case to support it. Preheat the oven to 200°C/400°F/Gas Mark 6 and bake blind for 10–15 minutes.

4. Remove from the oven and take out the foil. Fill with the meat mixture, packing it in tightly and levelling the top. Brush the top edge of the pastry with a little milk to glaze. Press the foil over the meat to cover it tightly and reduce the oven temperature to 180°C/350°F/Gas Mark 4. Cook for 2 hours or until the juices run clear when a skewer is pushed into the meat mixture. Remove from the oven, discard the foil and allow the pie to cool before removing it from the tin.

5. To make the topping: place the cranberries and sugar in a saucepan and cover with cold water. Heat until the sugar dissolves and the cranberries 'pop'. Remove from the heat, and drain. Arrange the cranberries over the top of the pie. Beat together the cranberry or redcurrant jelly and lemon juice until smooth and then heat until bubbling. Brush over the cranberries on top of the pie.

Pork and Cranberry Pie

BACON AND HAM

Bacon is the smoked or unsmoked flesh of a pig preserved by using curing salts. Whole, cured leg of pig is usually called gammon when eaten hot and ham when served cold. Some special hams, such as York and Bradenham, are cured and cooked according to traditional local methods. Honey-roast and Virginia-style are other special cures.

Bacon and ham joints

Collar
A large joint, usually divided into prime collar, middle collar and end collar. Sold boned and rolled; excellent boiling and roasting joints.

Forehock
Economical foreleg cut; fatty and on the bone. Boil or casserole.

Back
Usually cut into top back, short back and long back rashers, plus a small joint called the oyster cut. Top back can be cut into boneless bacon chops, or boned and rolled for boiling and casseroling.

Flank
The front end is cut into thin streaky rashers; it is also sold as a joint for boiling. Middle, through cut and long back rashers are cut from the back and the flank to give a mixture of lean and fat.

Gammon
The hind leg of the bacon pig, cut into four joints. Gammon hock is sold on the bone and is ideal for braising or making into soups and pies. Middle gammon is the prime joint and the best for boiling and roasting. Corner gammon and gammon slipper are best boiled or roasted. Thick gammon steaks and thin gammon rashers are cut from the middle gammon for frying and grilling.

Storing bacon and ham
Both have a longer storage life than fresh pork, due to the curing process; smoking will further increase it. Uncooked bacon joints and rashers will keep for up to ten days in the refrigerator. Unopened vacuum packs will store for much longer (check with the date on the pack) but, once opened, have the same storage life as loose bacon.

Freezing
Bacon and ham can be frozen, but the salt in them speeds up the rate at which fat turns rancid; therefore loose bacon and ham joints will only freeze for 1 month. Vacuum-packed joints can be frozen for up to 3 months and vacuum-packed rashers for 6 months.

BACON AND BLUE CHEESE RING

Serves 4–6

Choux pastry:
50 g (2 oz) butter
125 ml (¼ pint) cold water
65 g (2½ oz) strong plain flour
2 size 3 eggs
15 ml (1 tbsp) Bisto Powder
30 ml (2 tbsp) flaked almonds
Filling:
225 g (8 oz) gammon steak
50 g (2 oz) butter
1 leek, trimmed and sliced thinly

1 dessert apple, peeled, cored and cut
into small dice
15 ml (1 tbsp) caster sugar
1 avocado, peeled and cut into 1 cm
(½-inch) dice
15 ml (1 tbsp) lemon juice
250 ml (½ pint) white sauce, made
with Bisto White Sauce Granules as
directed
75 g (3 oz) Blue Stilton cheese,
crumbled

1. To make the choux pastry: dice the butter and place in a saucepan, with the water. Melt over a gentle heat, and then bring to the boil. Remove from the heat, tip in the flour and beat with a wooden spoon until the mixture leaves the sides of the pan. Beat the eggs with the Bisto Powder and add to the mixture a little at a time, beating well between additions.
2. Spoon the choux into a piping bag fitted with a 2 cm (¾-inch) plain or star nozzle and pipe an 18 cm (7-inch) ring on a dampened baking sheet.
3. Preheat the oven to 200°C/400°F/Gas Mark 6. Sprinkle the flaked almonds over the choux ring and bake for about 45 minutes until well browned. Remove from the oven and turn the ring over. Prick the base several times with a skewer and return to the oven, upside-down, for 5 minutes. Allow to cool on a wire rack, and then cut the ring in half through the centre and scrape out any uncooked pastry with a teaspoon.
4. To make the filling: grill the gammon steak for 3–4 minutes on each side until cooked. Cut into 1 cm (½-inch) dice.
5. Melt the butter in a frying-pan and fry the leek until soft. Add the apple and sprinkle with the caster sugar. Fry until lightly caramelised.
6. Place the gammon in a bowl and add the leek and apple mixture. Toss the avocado cubes in the lemon juice and add to the bowl. Stir in the white sauce and crumbled Stilton.
7. Increase the oven temperature to 220°C/425°F/Gas Mark 7. Place the bottom half of the choux ring on a baking sheet and spoon the filling over it. Top with the other half of the ring and place in the oven for 10 to 15 minutes until hot. Serve with a salad.

BACON AND BROCCOLI CRÊPES

Serves 4   ✱ *Without sauce*

Batter:
100 g (4 oz) plain flour
1 size 3 egg
1 egg yolk
250 ml (½ pint) milk
15 ml (1 tbsp) melted butter
15 ml (1 tbsp) chopped mixed fresh herbs
Filling:
30 ml (2 tbsp) oil
225 g (8 oz) bacon chop or gammon steak, cut into matchstick strips

225 g (8 oz) cooked broccoli, cut into tiny florets
100 g (4 oz) mushrooms, sliced
15 ml (1 tbsp) Bisto Powder
15 ml (1 tbsp) cornflour
250 ml (½ pint) cold water
30 ml (2 tbsp) double cream
500 g (1 lb) cooked chopped spinach
Sauce:
400 ml (¾ pint) cheese sauce, made with Bisto Cheese Sauce Granules
50 g (2 oz) grated Cheddar cheese
15 ml (1 tbsp) dry breadcrumbs

1. To make the batter: sift the flour into a bowl, make a well in the centre and put in the whole egg, egg yolk and half the milk. Draw the flour into the liquid, and then add the rest of the milk, the melted butter and herbs and beat or whisk until smooth and free of lumps. Leave to stand for 30 minutes.

2. To cook the crêpes: heat a 15 or 18 cm (6 or 7-inch) frying-pan and brush lightly with oil. Add about 30 ml (2 tbsp) of the batter and swirl to cover the base of the pan. Cook for about 1 minute or until the underside of the crêpe is golden brown; then flip over and cook the other side. Slide the crêpe out of the pan on to a plate lined with kitchen paper. Cook more crêpes in the same way until all the batter has been used, stacking the cooked crêpes on top of each other.

3. To make the filling: heat the oil in a pan and fry the bacon strips for about 5 minutes until lightly browned, stirring frequently. Remove with a draining spoon. Add the broccoli and the mushrooms to the pan and cook, stirring for 2 minutes. Return the bacon to the pan and sprinkle in the Bisto Powder and cornflour. Off the heat, blend in the cold water and then bring to the boil, stirring. Lower the heat and simmer for 5 minutes. Stir in the cream and remove from the heat.

4. Lightly grease a shallow, ovenproof dish and spread the spinach over the base. Divide the filling between the crêpes, roll up and place on top of the spinach, making two layers if necessary. Spoon the cheese sauce over and sprinkle with the Cheddar cheese and crumbs.

5. Set the oven at 190°C/375°F/Gas Mark 5. Cook the crêpes in the oven for 30 minutes until hot. Brown under a grill if liked.

Bacon and Blue Cheese Ring; Bacon and Broccoli Crêpes

HAM AND BEANS POT

Serves 6 ✳

*225 g (8 oz) black-eyed beans, soaked
in cold water overnight
350 g (12 oz) unsmoked gammon, cut
into 2.5 cm (1-inch) cubes and
soaked in cold water for 4 hours
30 ml (2 tbsp) oil
225 g (8 oz) herby pork sausages
2 leeks, trimmed and cut into 1 cm
(½-inch) lengths*

*2 × 400 g (14 oz) can of chopped
tomatoes
30 ml (2 tbsp) tomato purée
15 ml (1 tbsp) black treacle
250 ml (½ pint) gravy, made with Bisto
Rich Gravy Granules for Chicken as
directed
a small cauliflower, cut into florets*

1. Drain the beans and the gammon. Heat the oil in a large, heatproof pan and brown the sausages over a brisk heat on all sides. Remove and cut each sausage into 3 or 4 pieces.
2. Add the gammon and stir-fry for 2–3 minutes. Lower the heat, add the beans, sausages, leeks, tomatoes, tomato purée, black treacle and gravy to the pan and bring slowly to the boil.
3. Lower the heat and simmer gently, covered, for 1 hour. Add the cauliflower and cook for a further 30 minutes or until the beans are tender.

MARMALADE-BAKED GAMMON

Serves 8 ✳

*1.4 kg (3 lb) gammon or bacon joint,
soaked overnight
1 carrot, peeled
1 onion, peeled and stuck with
4 cloves
a bay leaf*

*30 ml (2 tbsp) orange marmalade
15 ml (1 tbsp) honey
30 ml (2 tbsp) Bisto Powder
5 ml (1 tsp) French mustard
125 ml (¼ pint) fresh orange juice*

1. Drain the joint and place in a saucepan. Cover with cold water, bring to the boil and simmer for 20 minutes. Drain and cover with fresh water. Add the carrot, onion and bay leaf and bring back to the boil. Simmer, keeping the joint submerged, for about 1 hour. Drain, reserving the liquid. Cut away the rind. Score the fat in a diamond pattern.
2. Preheat the oven to 200°C/400°F/Gas Mark 6. Lay the joint in a roasting tin. Mix together the marmalade, honey, Bisto Powder, mustard, orange juice and 250 ml (½ pint) of the cooking liquid. Pour over the joint and roast in the oven for 20 minutes, basting every 5 minutes.

Ham and Beans Pot; Marmalade-baked Gammon

3. Remove to a serving dish and keep warm. Bring the juices to the boil and reduce until syrupy. Serve in slices, with mashed potatoes and cabbage and spoon the sauce over.

POULTRY AND GAME

Poultry is a general term, covering domestic birds that are bred for the table. It includes chicken, duck, goose, guinea-fowl and turkey. The term 'game' is applied to wild birds and animals that are hunted; most have a 'close season', when shooting is forbidden. The only game not so protected is rabbits, pigeons and quails, which are available fresh all year.

Types of poultry and game

Chicken

Formerly a special occasion dish, chicken's wide availability and cheapness now make it a regular choice. Extremely versatile, chicken can be roasted, grilled, steamed, casseroled, poached, microwaved or stir-fried, and it is equally good eaten hot or cold. It will be complemented by most herbs and spices and also team up well with more unlikely partners like nuts and dried fruits. Chicken freezes well but, as with all poultry and feathered game, it must be completely defrosted before cooking. Chicken should only ever be eaten well cooked.

When buying a chicken, look for evenly-coloured, creamy skin that has no blemishes or discoloured patches. A chicken should be moist and plump and any plastic wrap surrounding it should be unbroken. Unwrap, loosely cover and refrigerate in a separate container.

Turkey

Turkeys are on sale all year round, not just at Christmas time! Turkey joints mean you can enjoy the meat without having to live off a whole turkey for days and days. Whole turkeys should have plump breasts, black legs, short necks and flesh that is white with a pale blue tinge.

Duck

Duck is a fatty bird that is best roasted. It will not serve as many people as a chicken of the same weight; a 2 kg (4 lb) duck will only serve 2–3 people. Look for a plump breast, soft underbill, and pliable feet. It is now possible to buy *magret de canard*, the breast joint of a French-bred duck that is very meaty and full-flavoured. The flesh is firm and not too fatty and is excellent grilled or stir-fried. The French usually eat *magret* rare.

Goose

Considered by many to be the finest of all poultry, roast goose is now making a comeback on our Christmas dining tables. It is a fatty bird, with creamy-white flesh that has a slightly gamey flavour. It will serve fewer people than a similar weight of chicken or turkey. Choose a young bird with soft yellow feet and legs.

Guinea-fowl

The flesh is tender and has a flavour similar to young pheasant. It can be roasted, braised or casseroled and an average-sized bird will serve three people.

Game

Partridge are available from September 1st to the end of January. Young partridge can be roasted; older ones are best casseroled. Serve 1 per person. **Pheasants** are sold as a brace or singly; the hen usually has the best flavour. Available from October 1st to the end of January, they are best in the six weeks or so leading up to Christmas when they are young, tender and ideal for roasting. Older pheasants are best casseroled. One pheasant serves 2–3. **Pigeons** are available all year, but at their best from August to October. Young ones can be roasted or grilled; more mature ones are best casseroled or made into a pie. Serve 1 per person. Casserole, roast or barbecue **quail**, but don't overcook or they will dry out. They are available

fresh all year. Serve 1 per person. Young **hares** can be roasted whole and will serve 4–6, older ones are better in casseroles, although the saddle can be roasted. Available from August 1st to the end of March, they are best from October onwards. Wild **rabbit** can have a slightly gamey flavour, but the more usual domesticated ones have a flavour that is more like chicken. Sold whole or jointed, they are available all year and can be roasted or casseroled. The best **venison** meat is from the young male deer. The flesh is lean and rich dark red, with firm, white fat. Venison is sold in joints, the best cuts being the leg and saddle, plus loin chops, neck cutlets and shoulder for braising. It is available from June to January.

CREAMY CHICKEN AND ALMOND CURRY

Serves 4　　　　　　　　　　　　　　　　　　　　　★ *Without yogurt*

60 ml (4 tbsp) oil
4 chicken legs
2 onions, sliced thinly
100 g (4 oz) ground almonds
15 ml (1 tbsp) curry paste
250 ml (½ pint) gravy, made with Bisto
　Rich Gravy Granules for Chicken

5 ml (1 tsp) cornflour
125 ml (5 fl oz) natural yogurt
To serve:
30 ml (2 tbsp) toasted flaked almonds
chopped fresh mint

1. Heat the oil and brown the chicken legs; turn once. Remove.
2. Add the onions and soften over a low heat; increase the heat and cook until golden. Stir in the ground almonds, lower the heat and cook for 1 minute. Stir in the curry paste and cook for a further 1 minute.
3. Replace the chicken legs, pour in the gravy and bring to the boil. Lower the heat and simmer gently, covered, for 1¼ hours or until the chicken is tender, stirring occasionally.
4. Transfer the chicken to a serving dish. Keep warm. Blend the cornflour and yogurt; stir into the pan, off the heat. Bring to the boil, stirring. Simmer for 30 seconds and then pour over the chicken.
5. Sprinkle with the almonds and mint and serve with rice.

ROAST CHICKEN WITH LEMON AND LEEK STUFFING

Serves 4

When I was a child, I always thought of roast chicken as the ultimate treat for our family lunch on Sundays; even though chicken is now a much more commonplace meal, I still enjoy it just as much. Roast chicken lends itself to all sorts of tasty stuffings and I particularly like this tangy mixture of lemon and herbs.

1.4 kg (3 lb) oven-ready chicken
50 g (2 oz) melted butter
5 ml (1 tsp) dried thyme
Stuffing:
1 leek, trimmed and sliced thinly
25 g (1 oz) butter
15 ml (1 tbsp) ground almonds
15 ml (1 tbsp) Bisto Powder

175 g (6 oz) fresh white breadcrumbs
15 ml (1 tbsp) snipped fresh chives
5 ml (1 tsp) dried tarragon
grated rind and juice of 1 lemon
1 size 3 egg, beaten
To serve:
gravy made with Bisto Rich Gravy
*   Granules for Chicken*

1. Preheat the oven to 180°C/350°F/Gas Mark 4. Wipe the chicken inside and out and place in a roasting tin. Brush with the melted butter and sprinkle over the thyme. Roast for 50 minutes, basting from time to time.
2. To make the stuffing: fry the leek in the butter until soft. Stir in the ground almonds and Bisto and cook for 1 minute. Remove from the heat and stir in the breadcrumbs, chives, tarragon, rind and juice of the lemon and the beaten egg to bind. Roll the stuffing into small balls.
3. When the chicken has been roasting for 50 minutes, arrange the stuffing balls around it and return it to the oven. Roast for a further 30 minutes or until the juices of the chicken run clear when the thickest part of a leg joint is pierced with a skewer.
4. Remove the chicken and place it on a warmed carving plate; put the stuffing balls around it.
5. Skim the fat from the roasting tin and pour in the Bisto gravy. Bring to the boil and strain it into a gravy boat. Carve or joint chicken and serve with roast potatoes and mixed vegetables.

Roast Chicken with Lemon and Leek Stuffing

CORIANDER AND CHICKEN PIES

Serves 4   ✱

Pastry:
100 g (4 oz) plain flour
100 g (4 oz) wholemeal flour
75 g (3 oz) block margarine
50 g (2 oz) ground almonds
1 size 3 egg, beaten
cold water to mix
Filling:
30 ml (2 tbsp) oil
2 boneless chicken breasts, skinned
    and cut into 1 cm (½-inch) cubes
6 spring onions, trimmed and sliced
    thinly

1 small green pepper, de-seeded and
    chopped into small dice
50 g (2 oz) button mushrooms, sliced
15 ml (1 tbsp) chopped fresh coriander
125 ml (¼ pint) gravy, made with Bisto
    Rich Gravy Granules for Chicken as
    directed
30 ml (2 tbsp) double cream
To glaze:
beaten egg
25 g (1 oz) finely chopped walnuts

1. To make the pastry: sift the plain flour into a bowl and add the wholemeal flour. Cut the margarine into small pieces and rub in until the mixture resembles fine breadcrumbs. Stir in the ground almonds, egg and enough cold water to make a firm but not sticky dough. Knead lightly on a floured board until smooth; then wrap in cling film or greaseproof paper and chill for 30 minutes.

2. To make the filling: heat the oil and stir-fry the chicken for 3 minutes. Remove with a draining spoon and set aside. Add the spring onions, pepper and mushrooms to the pan and fry until the onions are soft. Return the chicken to the pan, stir in the coriander and add the gravy. Bring to the boil; allow the sauce to bubble and reduce until thick. Remove from the heat and stir in the cream. Leave to cool.

3. Preheat the oven to 200°C/400°F/Gas Mark 6. Roll out the pastry thinly on a lightly floured surface and cut out eight 10 cm (4-inch) rounds. Place on a baking sheet and brush the edges with cold water. Divide the filling in eight and pile into the centre of each pastry round.

4. Re-roll the remaining pastry and cut out lids large enough to cover the filling – about 12.5 cm (5 inches) across. Cover the filling with the lids, fold over the pastry edges together to seal and flute the edges. Cut a hole in the top of each pie and decorate with pastry trimmings, fixing in place by brushing with cold water.

5. Brush with beaten egg and sprinkle with the walnuts. Bake for 20 minutes, and then lower the heat to 180°C/350°F/Gas Mark 4 and cook for a further 15 minutes until golden brown.

6. Serve with jacket potatoes and salad.

Coriander and Chicken Pies

CHEESY CHICKEN LASAGNE

Serves 4   ✱

4–6 sheets of lasagne, cooked
Chicken layer:
30 ml (2 tbsp) oil
225 g (8 oz) chicken breast, skinned
   and minced
100 g (4 oz) cooked chopped ham
15 ml (1 tbsp) Bisto Powder
400 g (14 oz) can of chopped tomatoes
5 ml (1 tsp) dried oregano

Broccoli layer:
225 g (8 oz) broccoli, cut into small
   florets
a pinch of ground nutmeg
225 g (8 oz) ricotta cheese
125 ml (5 fl oz) natural yogurt
2 size 3 eggs
White sauce:
2 leeks, trimmed and sliced thinly
25 g (1 oz) butter
50 g (2 oz) Bisto White Sauce Granules
50 g (2 oz) grated Gruyère cheese

1. Drain the lasagne and pat dry on kitchen paper.
2. Heat the oil in a pan and fry the chicken for 2–3 minutes until pale. Stir in the chopped ham, Bisto Powder, chopped tomatoes and their juice and oregano. Bring to the boil, and then lower the heat and simmer for 10 minutes.
3. Cook the broccoli florets in boiling salted water until tender; then drain, refresh and chop roughly. Season with the nutmeg. Beat together the ricotta cheese, yogurt and eggs until smooth, and then stir the broccoli into the mixture until combined.
4. Sauté the leeks in the butter until soft but not browned. Make up the Sauce Granules with 250 ml (½ pint) boiling water, according to directions. Stir the leeks into the sauce.
5. Preheat the oven to 180°C/350°F/Gas Mark 4. Spoon half the chicken into a rectangular 25 × 15 cm (10 × 6-inch) ovenproof dish and top with half the lasagne. Spoon a broccoli layer over the lasagne and add the remaining lasagne. Cover with the remaining chicken and spoon the white sauce over. Sprinkle with the grated cheese.
6. Bake for 35–40 minutes until bubbling. Serve with a salad.

Cheesy Chicken Lasagne

CHINESE CHICKEN STIR-FRY

Serves 4

45 ml (3 tbsp) oil
350 g (12 oz) boneless chicken
    breasts, skinned and cut into
    bite-sized pieces
2 red peppers, de-seeded and sliced
8 spring onions, trimmed and sliced
    diagonally
4 sticks of celery, sliced
1 cm (½-inch) piece of root ginger,
    peeled and chopped very finely

1 clove of garlic, crushed
125 ml (¼ pint) water
20 ml (4 tsp) Bisto Rich Gravy
    Granules for Chicken
15 ml (1 tbsp) soy sauce
100 g (4 oz) beansprouts
1 size 3 egg
15 g (½ oz) butter

1. Heat the oil in a wok or large frying-pan and stir-fry the chicken for 5–6 minutes until just cooked through. Remove and keep warm.

2. Add the peppers, spring onions, celery, ginger and garlic to the pan and stir-fry for 4–5 minutes, or until the vegetables are tender-crisp. Remove and keep warm.

3. Add the water, Bisto Gravy Granules and soy sauce to the pan. Boil for a few moments and then add the beansprouts and return the chicken and vegetables to the pan. Toss over the heat for 1–2 minutes until well combined. Transfer to a serving dish and keep warm.

4. Beat the egg with 15 ml (1 tbsp) water. Melt the butter in a small frying-pan and when foaming pour in the egg mixture. Cook until set and lightly browned underneath and then transfer to a plate and cut into thin strips.

5. Top the stir-fry with the omelette strips and serve at once.

Creamy Chicken and Almond Curry (page 63); Chinese Chicken Stir-fry

CHICKEN, AVOCADO AND SWEETCORN TOSTADAS

Serves 4

30 ml (2 tbsp) oil
1 large onion, chopped
750 g (1½ lb) boneless chicken
  breasts, skinned and cut into
  bite-sized pieces
10 ml (2 tsp) ground cumin
15 ml (1 tbsp) Bisto Powder
15 ml (1 tbsp) tomato purée
198 g (7 oz) can of sweetcorn kernels
  with peppers, drained

125 ml (¼ pint) carton of fresh soured
  cream
8 tostada shells
1 small lettuce, shredded
100 g (4 oz) Cheddar cheese, grated
½ avocado, peeled and sliced
1 small onion, peeled and sliced into
  rings
2 tomatoes, cut into small dice
To serve:
lemon or lime wedges

1. Heat the oil in a pan and sauté the onion until soft. Add the chicken pieces and stir-fry until pale coloured. Stir in the ground cumin and cook for 1 minute, and then stir in the Bisto Powder, tomato purée, sweetcorn and soured cream. Simmer for 15 minutes, stirring occasionally.
2. Preheat the oven to 140°C/275°F/Gas Mark 1. Place the tostadas in the oven for 5–10 minutes, until warm.
3. To assemble: divide the lettuce between the hot tostadas. Top with the chicken and sweetcorn mixture, grated cheese, avocado slices, onion rings and chopped tomato. Serve immediately and squeeze the lemon or lime wedges over the topping.

COQ AU VIN

Serves 4   ✱

4 chicken legs
30 ml (2 tbsp) plain flour
60 ml (4 tbsp) oil
100 g (4 oz) streaky bacon, chopped
16 button onions, peeled
175 g (6 oz) button mushrooms
2 cloves of garlic, crushed

20 ml (4 tsp) Bisto Powder
250 ml (½ pint) cold water
250 ml (½ pint) dry red wine
15 ml (1 tbsp) tomato purée
a bay leaf
pepper to taste

1. Wipe the chicken joints with kitchen paper and coat in flour.
2. Heat the oil in a large frying-pan and fry the bacon and onions until the onions are golden brown, stirring frequently. Transfer the bacon and onions to a large casserole. Add the chicken pieces to the frying-pan and

Coq au Vin; Chicken, Avocado and Sweetcorn Tostadas

fry for about 10 minutes until brown, turning once or twice. Transfer the chicken to the casserole.

3. Preheat the oven to 150°C/300°F/Gas Mark 2. Add the mushrooms and garlic to the frying-pan and fry for 1 minute. Blend the Bisto Powder with a little of the water until smooth and add it to the pan with the remaining water, red wine and tomato purée. Bring to the boil, stirring, and pour the sauce over the contents of the casserole. Add the bay leaf to the casserole and season with pepper to taste. Cover and cook in the oven for 1½ hours or until the chicken pieces are tender. Remove the bay leaf.

GALANTINE OF CHICKEN WITH FRUIT AND NUTS

Serves 8 ✱

75 g (3 oz) bulgar wheat
25 g (1 oz) butter
1 onion, chopped finely
1 green pepper, de-seeded and
  chopped finely
15 ml (1 tbsp) Bisto Powder
25 g (1 oz) no-need-to-soak dried
  apricots, chopped

25 g (1 oz) sultanas
50 g (2 oz) pistachio nuts, chopped
350 g (12 oz) pork sausage meat
2.5 ml (½ tsp) ground cinnamon
2 size 3 eggs, beaten
1.8 kg (4 lb) chicken, boned
8 pitted prunes

1. Place the bulgar wheat in a bowl. Cover with boiling water and leave to stand, covered, for 30 minutes. Drain and squeeze the wheat to extract as much water as possible. Set aside.

2. Melt the butter in a pan and soften the onion and green pepper. Stir in the Bisto Powder, apricots, sultanas and nuts and cook for 1 minute. Remove from the heat and cool.

3. Mix the bulgar wheat and onion mixture with the sausage meat and cinnamon. Stir in the beaten eggs to bind.

4. Open out the chicken on a board, skin-side down. Spoon half the stuffing mixture into the centre of the chicken and put the prunes in a line down the centre. Spoon the rest of the stuffing on top to form a long sausage coming to about 2.5 cm (1 inch) of the edge. Fold the ends of the chicken up and over the stuffing.

5. Sew up the skin using a darning needle threaded with thin string. Place the chicken roll on a rack in a roasting tin.

6. Preheat the oven to 200°C/400°F/Gas Mark 6. Roast for 1½–1¾ hours, or until the juices run clear when roll is pierced with a skewer, basting occasionally.

7. Allow to cool completely before slicing. Serve with a selection of salads and new potatoes.

Galantine of Chicken with Fruit and Nuts

TRADITIONAL ROAST TURKEY

Turkey doesn't have to be just for Christmas – it's a good choice for any time of the year when you have a party to feed. If you allow about 500 g (1 lb) of turkey per person there will be some left over for sandwiches the next day. You can prepare the turkey for the oven the day before, filling the neck of the bird with stuffing and trussing the legs with string so it keeps its shape while roasting.

Frozen turkeys

It is essential that a frozen turkey is thawed completely before cooking. If you have room you can thaw it in the bottom of the refrigerator, but this will take approximately twice as long as thawing at cool room temperature. Approximate thawing times at room temperature are given below.

Thawing times of turkey at room temperature

Weight of turkey	Thawing time
2.3–3.6 kg (5–8 lb)	15–18 hours
3.6–5 kg (8–11 lb)	18–20 hours
5–6.8 kg (11–15 lb)	20–24 hours
6.8–9 kg (15–20 lb)	24–30 hours

Stand the frozen turkey in a roasting tin and allow it to thaw sufficiently so that you can cut away any outer plastic wrapping. Remove this and cover the turkey loosely with foil or cling film. Leave until completely thawed, pouring off any liquid from the tin from time to time. A turkey is completely thawed when there are no ice crystals left in the body cavity.

Roasting

Weigh the turkey after it has been stuffed and calculate the cooking time from the chart. Tuck the wing pinions under the body, securing the flap of neck skin under them, and lift the turkey into a roasting tin. Brush the skin all over with melted butter or oil and cover with foil or with a double thickness of muslin that has been soaked in melted butter. Some cooks feel that covering a turkey with foil causes the bird to steam rather than roast, but as long as the foil is removed about an hour before the end of cooking and the turkey basted frequently during that final hour, the end result is as good as any other cooking method. If you cover your turkey with muslin, remove this 45 minutes before the end of the cooking time. To test if the flesh is cooked, push a skewer between the breast and thigh of the turkey, or into the thickest part of the leg; the juices should run clear. When it is done, remove the turkey from the oven and cover with foil. Allow to stand for 15–20 minutes in a warm place before you carve it, to allow the juices to flow back into the body and make carving easier.

Traditional Roast Turkey

Roasting times for turkey at 170°C/325°F/Gas Mark 3

Weight of turkey	Roasting time
2.7–4.5 kg (6–10 lb)	3–3¾ hours
4.5–6.3 kg (10–14 lb)	3¾–4¼ hours
6.3–8.2 kg (14–18 lb)	4¼–4¾ hours

Any leftover meat can be frozen on the bone, or be carved into large chunks. Wrap and seal well to prevent freezer 'burn' and use within 2 months. Uncooked turkey will freeze for up to 6 months.

Traditional accompaniments

Bacon rolls: Streaky bacon is best for these. Allow 25 g (1 oz) bacon per person, remove the rind and bones and cut each rasher in half. Stretch the bacon with the back of a knife, roll up and secure with a wooden cocktail stick. Roast around the turkey for the final 45 minutes. **Chipolatas:** Twist each chipolata in the centre to give two small, cocktail-size sausages. Roast with the bacon rolls for the final 45 minutes. **Bread sauce:** Peel a large onion and stud it with four whole cloves. Place in a saucepan with a bay leaf and a blade of mace and pour over 400 ml (¾ pint) of milk. Bring to the boil, remove from the heat and cover the pan. Leave to infuse for 30 minutes. Discard the cloves, bay leaf and mace. Finely chop the onion and add to the milk with 100 g (4 oz) fresh bread-crumbs, salt and pepper. Simmer gently for 10 minutes and then stir in 25 g (1 oz) butter.

Turkey stuffings: Most people have developed their own family favourites over the years but stuffings based on herbs, chestnuts and sharp-flavoured lemon rind seem to be the most enduringly popular.

Other traditional accompaniments are roast potatoes, sprouts and chestnuts, carrots and cranberry sauce. Make a rich gravy with Bisto Powder, blended with water or stock made from the turkey giblets, and added to the skimmed cooking juices in the roasting tin.

TRADITIONAL ROAST PHEASANT WITH MADEIRA SAUCE

Serves 6

Pheasants can be rather dry, but covering the breasts of the birds with bacon while they cook keeps the flesh tender and succulent. The Madeira sauce can be made ahead and reheated when needed – add the cooking juices from the pheasant to it just before serving.

2 oven-ready pheasants
8 rashers of streaky bacon, rind and
*   bones removed*
50 g (2 oz) unsalted butter, melted
5 ml (1 tsp) Bisto Powder

Madeira sauce:
15 ml (1 tbsp) oil
1 onion, chopped finely
400 ml (¾ pint) gravy, made with
*   20 ml (4 tsp) Bisto Rich Gravy*
*   Granules for Chicken and 400 ml*
*   (¾ pint) boiling water*
50 ml (2 fl oz) Sercial (dry) Madeira

1. Preheat the oven to 220°C/425°F/Gas Mark 7. Rinse the pheasants in cold water, pull out any remaining feathers and check that no shot is still lodged in the flesh. Wipe the birds with kitchen paper. Truss the legs together with thin string and place the pheasants side-by-side in a roasting tin. Place the bacon over the breasts of the birds and secure with wooden cocktail sticks.

2. Mix together the melted butter and Bisto Powder and brush over the birds. Roast for 10 minutes; then lower the heat to 190°C/375°F/Gas Mark 5, and roast for a further 35 minutes.

3. Remove the bacon and baste with the cooking juices. Roast for another 10 minutes or until the juices run clear when a skewer is pushed through the thickest part of the leg joint. Transfer to a carving dish and remove the trussing string. Keep warm.

4. To make the Madeira sauce: heat the oil in a saucepan and fry the onion gently until soft and starting to brown. Add the gravy and Madeira and simmer for 10 minutes until reduced by about a third. Skim excess fat from the cooking juices in the roasting tin, pour in the Madeira sauce and bring to the boil, scraping the bottom of the tin with a spatula. Allow to bubble for 1–2 minutes and strain into a warmed gravy boat.

5. Serve the pheasants garnished with tail feathers, fried apple rings (if liked) and a bunch of watercress. Accompany with game chips, bread sauce and the Madeira sauce.

HONEY ROAST DUCK WITH MANGO SAUCE

Serves 4

Duck seems to me the ideal meat for so many oriental-style dishes because its rich taste is such a good partner for the sweetly-sharp sauces of Chinese and other Far-Eastern cuisines. This would make a good dish for a dinner party: serve it with boiled or fried rice mixed with cooked peas, peppers, corn and spring onions and a salad of bitter continental lettuces such as radicchio, frisée or feuille de chêne.

2–2.5 kg (4–4½ lb) oven-ready duck
salt
45 ml (3 tbsp) clear honey
30 ml (2 tbsp) sesame seeds

Sauce:
1 ripe mango
15 ml (1 tbsp) soy sauce
15 ml (1 tbsp) Bisto Powder
125 ml (¼ pint) cold water
125 ml (¼ pint) ginger beer

1. Wipe the duck and remove any giblets. Place the duck on a rack in a roasting tin, breast-side up, and prick the skin of the duck with a skewer – this will make it self-basting while it cooks. Rub the skin of the duck all over with salt.
2. Preheat the oven to 180°C/350°F/Gas Mark 4 and roast the duck for 30 minutes per 500 g (1 lb). 20 minutes before the end of cooking time, increase the oven temperature to 200°C/400°F/Gas Mark 6. Brush the honey over the duck and sprinkle with the sesame seeds.
3. To make the sauce: cut the mango flesh away from the fibrous centre stone and peel it. Finely chop the flesh and mix with the soy sauce, or liquidise the mango and soy in a food processor until smooth. Blend the Bisto Powder with the cold water. Heat the ginger beer until simmering and then stir in the Bisto Powder mixture. Bring to the boil, stirring, add the mango and soy sauce and heat through.
4. Carve or joint the duck and serve with the sauce spooned alongside the meat.

Honey Roast Duck with Mango Sauce;
Traditional Roast Pheasant with Madeira Sauce

ROAST GOOSE WITH SAGE, ONION AND APPLE STUFFING

Serves 8

Geese seem to personify the festive spirit of Christmas and in recent years they have been gaining in popularity over the previously ubiquitous turkey. The meat of a goose is fairly rich and fatty, and so a sharp, fruity stuffing will complement it very well.

4.5 kg (10 lb) oven-ready goose
Stuffing:
2 large onions, chopped finely
25 g (1 oz) butter
15 ml (1 tbsp) Bisto Powder
225 g (8 oz) fresh brown breadcrumbs

30 ml (2 tbsp) chopped fresh sage or
*   15 ml (1 tbsp) dried sage*
grated rind and juice of 1 lemon
2 dessert apples, peeled, cored and
*   chopped into small dice*
2 size 3 eggs, beaten

1. Remove the giblets from the goose and any lumps of fat inside the bird. Rub the skin of the bird with salt.
2. To make the stuffing: fry the onions in the butter until soft, and stir in the Bisto Powder. Remove from the heat and add the breadcrumbs, sage, lemon rind and juice and apples. Bind the stuffing with the beaten eggs. Allow to cool, and use to stuff the goose. Truss the goose with thin string, stand on a rack set in a roasting tin and cover with foil.
3. Preheat the oven to 180°C/350°F/Gas Mark 4. Roast the goose for 25–30 minutes per 500 g (1 lb), removing the foil for the last 30 minutes so the skin will brown.
4. Serve with gravy made from Bisto Powder and water added to the juices from the roasting pan (tip the fat off first). Accompany with the stuffing, roast or boiled potatoes, green vegetables and redcurrant jelly.

Roast Goose with Sage, Onion and Apple Stuffing

OFFAL

Offal is the unattractive word that describes those parts of pigs, sheep and cattle which are cut away from the carcase when it is prepared for sale and which are not classified as cuts of meat. It's worth experimenting with some of the more unusual types, like sweetbreads, hearts and tripe. Offal is not only very nutritious, it's also lean and there's very little waste, and it can be bought in small quantities: useful for single people. Offal should preferably be cooked the same day you buy it, and certainly within 24 hours.

Types of offal

Tail
Oxtail is usually the only type sold and it is ready-skinned and jointed. It needs long, slow casseroling, but makes excellent stews and soups.

Tongue
Ox and lamb's tongues are fairly widely available. Lamb's tongues are small, only weighing about 225 g (8 oz) each, and are usually braised. An ox tongue needs slow cooking to tenderise it. It can be eaten hot with a port wine or Madeira sauce, or pressed and served cold.

Liver
The best is calves', followed by lamb's, pig's and ox in that order. Calves' and lamb's liver can be grilled, fried or braised. Pig's and ox livers are much more strongly flavoured and are better used in stews and casseroles, or minced and added to pâtés.

Sweetbreads
Two portions of the thymus gland taken from the throat and chest cavity of the calf and lamb. They are sold by the 500 g (1 lb) to serve 3 or 4 people. They can be used in a variety of dishes such as braises and casseroles or simmered in a rich sauce.

Tripe
Tripe is the stomach lining of an ox (but don't let that put you off!). There are three types: 'blanket', taken from the smooth first stomach of the animal; 'honeycomb', from the second stomach; and 'thick seam' from the third. All should be thick, firm and white and they all taste the same. Tripe is sold bleached (dressed) and partly cooked. It can be stewed, boiled in milk, or sliced and deep-fried. Allow about 175 g (6 oz) per person.

Kidney
Ox (for steak and kidney pudding and pie), lamb's and pig's kidneys are all available. Kidneys from the latter two animals should be cooked quickly or they will become tough.

Heart
Probably one of the leanest foods around. Pig's or lamb's hearts are best stuffed and then pot-roasted or casseroled as the meat is dense and fairly tough.

Brains
Brains have a delicate flavour and are usually sold in sets. One set of lamb's brains will serve 1, a set of calves' or ox brains, 2.

LIVER AND BACON PIE

Serves 6

Pastry:
175 g (6 oz) plain flour
25 g (1 oz) ground hazelnuts
25 g (1 oz) medium oatmeal
100 g (4 oz) butter or block margarine
about 30 ml (2 tbsp) cold water to mix
Filling:
12 baby onions, peeled
45 ml (3 tbsp) oil
2 sticks of celery, sliced

175 g (6 oz) streaky bacon, rind and
bones removed, and chopped
100 g (4 oz) tiny button mushrooms
600 g (1¼ lb) lamb's liver, cut into
thin strips
250 ml (½ pint) gravy, made with Bisto
Rich Gravy Granules as directed
To glaze:
beaten egg

1. To make the pastry: sift the flour into a bowl. Stir in the ground hazelnuts and oatmeal. Rub in the butter or margarine until the mixture resembles fine breadcrumbs, and then add enough water to make a soft, but not sticky, dough. Knead lightly on a floured surface until smooth, and then wrap in cling film or greaseproof paper and chill for 1 hour.

2. To make the filling: blanch the onions in boiling, salted water for 5 minutes; then drain. Heat the oil in a frying-pan and fry the onions until lightly browned. Remove and set aside.

3. Add the celery and bacon to the pan and fry until the bacon fat is transparent. Stir in the mushrooms and cook for a further 2 minutes. Remove from the pan and set aside.

4. Add the liver to the pan, with a little more oil if necessary, and stir-fry for 2–3 minutes. Pour in the gravy, return the vegetables and bacon to the pan and bring to the boil. Remove from the heat and spoon the mixture into a 750 ml (1½-pint) pie dish. Allow to cool.

5. Roll out the pastry on a lightly floured surface and cut a 2.5 cm (1-inch) strip to line the edge of the pie dish. Brush the strip with cold water and then cover the filling with pastry. Press the edges together to seal and flute if liked. Decorate the top with pastry trimmings, fixing them in place by brushing with cold water. Cut a small hole in the centre to allow steam to escape.

6. Preheat the oven to 200°C/400°F/Gas Mark 6. Brush the pastry with beaten egg to glaze and set the pie on a baking sheet. Bake for 30–35 minutes until well browned.

SAGE AND ORANGE LIVER

Serves 4

60 ml (4 tbsp) oil
8 spring onions, trimmed and cut into
    5 cm (2-inch) lengths
500 g (1 lb) calves' liver, sliced thinly
30 ml (2 tbsp) plain flour
15 ml (1 tbsp) Bisto Powder

15 ml (1 tbsp) ground almonds
15 ml (1 tbsp) chopped fresh sage
30 ml (2 tbsp) fresh orange juice
To garnish:
orange slices
fresh sage leaves

1. Heat 15 ml (1 tbsp) of the oil in a frying-pan and fry the onions until lightly browned, stirring frequently. Remove and keep warm.
2. Remove any ducts or tubes from the liver. Mix together the flour, Bisto Powder and almonds and coat both sides of the liver slices.
3. Using the rest of the oil, fry the liver for 2–3 minutes on each side or until the slices are still just pink in the centre.
4. Return the onions to the pan, add the sage and orange juice and allow to bubble for 1 minute.
5. Garnish the liver with orange slices and fresh sage leaves.

LIVER AND BACON STIR-FRY

Serves 4

350 g (12 oz) lamb's liver, sliced thinly
15 ml (1 tbsp) Bisto Powder
15 ml (1 tbsp) plain flour
about 60 ml (4 tbsp) oil
175 g (6 oz) back bacon, rind and
    bones removed and rashers cut into
    2.5 cm (1-inch) pieces

1 onion, sliced
1 red pepper, de-seeded and sliced
100 g (4 oz) mange-tout
60 ml (4 tbsp) dry vermouth or dry
    white wine
5 ml (1 tsp) dried mixed herbs

1. Toss the liver in the Bisto Powder and plain flour until well coated.
2. Heat the oil in a wok or large frying-pan and fry the bacon and onion until they are transparent and starting to brown. Add the pepper and mange-tout and stir-fry for a further 3–4 minutes until the pepper is still just crisp. Remove and keep warm.
3. Add a little more oil to the pan if necessary and stir-fry the liver for 2–3 minutes. Add the vermouth or wine and herbs and allow to bubble for a few seconds. Return the bacon and vegetables to the pan and turn together over the heat for a further 1 minute. Serve at once.

Liver and Bacon Pie; Liver and Bacon Stir-fry; Sage and Orange Liver

FAGGOTS

Serves 4 ※

350 g (12 oz) pig's liver, minced
175 g (6 oz) streaky pork, rind and
  bones removed, minced
1 onion, chopped finely
a pinch of ground nutmeg

10 ml (2 tsp) mixed dried herbs
15 ml (1 tbsp) Bisto Powder
50 g (2 oz) fresh white or brown
  breadcrumbs
1 size 3 egg, beaten

1. Preheat the oven to 180°C/350°F/Gas Mark 4.
2. Mix all the ingredients together in a large bowl until evenly blended.
3. With wet hands, divide the mixture into 8 equal-sized portions and shape into balls.
4. Place in a shallow, ovenproof dish greased with oil or melted lard and cover the dish with foil.
5. Cook in the oven for 1 hour or until browned.

RICH KIDNEY BRAISE

Serves 4 ※

8 chipolata sausages
30 ml (2 tbsp) oil
8 button onions, peeled
8 lamb's kidneys, cored and halved
2 courgettes, sliced diagonally

20 ml (4 tsp) Bisto Powder
250 ml (½ pint) brown ale or water
To garnish:
2 slices of white bread
oil for shallow-frying

1. Grill the sausages until browned on all sides. Remove from heat and cut each one into three.
2. Heat the oil in a deep frying-pan and fry the onions until lightly browned. Remove with a draining spoon.
3. Add the kidneys to the pan and fry over a brisk heat for 20–30 seconds on each side to seal. Remove kidneys from pan and discard any oil remaining in it.
4. Return the onions to the pan, add the courgette slices and sausages and add the Bisto Powder and brown ale or water. Bring to the boil, stirring, lower the heat and return the kidneys to the pan. Cover and simmer gently for 30 minutes.
5. To prepare the garnish: cut the crusts from the slices of bread and cut each slice into four triangles. Heat the oil and fry the bread until golden brown. Drain and serve with the kidneys.

Rich Kidney Braise; Faggots

MEAT AND THE MICROWAVE

Microwave cookery can save time, effort and money, but many cooks are reluctant to use microwave ovens to cook meat, in case an expensive cut turns out dry, tasteless and pale in colour. Successful meat cookery in a microwave is quite possible, however, providing you are careful to follow the correct procedures.

Points to remember when cooking meat by microwave

● When preparing meat cut it into even-sized pieces; choose steaks or chops of similar size so they cook evenly.

● Arrange joints such as cutlets or chicken drumsticks in a circle, with the thinnest parts of the food towards the centre. Place burgers or meatballs in a circle, again to promote even cooking.

● Avoid seasoning meat with salt before microwaving, as this will toughen it during cooking.

● Use containers made of a non-metallic material such as glass, china (without a gold or silver decorative edge), earthenware, plastic or special microwave dishes, so the microwaves can pass directly through the dish to the food. Although containers do not become hot during microwaving, they can become hot by heat being transferred from cooked food, so protect your hand with an oven glove when removing a hot dish.

● Choose regular-shaped containers, with rounded corners and straight sides, that will promote even cooking.

● Where a recipe specifies that food should be covered, this is to prevent liquid spattering the inside of the oven and to quicken the cooking process. Non-PVC cling film, pierced or rolled back at the corner, or a non-metallic plate, make effective lids. Remember to take care when removing a lid from a cooked dish, as steam can cause nasty burns.

● Prick sausages before microwaving, to allow pressure that builds up under the skin to escape.

● Although metal dishes should not be used, very small pieces of aluminium foil can be used to shield thin parts of food, such as chicken wing tips or bone ends of roasts, to prevent them burning.

● As with conventional cooking, economical cuts of meat need to be microwaved for a longer period of time and at a lower power output than prime cuts.

● When cooking meat in a sauce, select a deep cooking dish; if a sauce is thinly spread it will dehydrate and dry up during cooking. Stir frequently to ensure even heating.

● Fasten roasting bags with string or a non-metallic tie, and cut a small slit in the bag to allow steam to escape.

● A special meat thermometer for use in a microwave oven, or the electronic probe provided with some ovens, will calculate accurately

when a large joint is cooked. Never use a metal meat thermometer in the microwave.
• Allow food to come to room temperature first, rather than microwaving it straight from the refrigerator: it will take less time to heat up.

Browning meat in the microwave

Most cooks feel that the main disadvantage of cooking meat in a microwave is that the mouthwatering, brown succulence of a joint roasted in a conventional oven can't be achieved. Joints over about 2 kg (4 lb) will begin to brown naturally in a microwave as their longer cooking time means the surface of the meat has a prolonged exposure to dry, hot air. However, there are several easy and tasty ways to help overcome this browning problem. One simple way is to sprinkle Bisto Powder over small meat cuts like chops or steaks. As the meat cooks in the microwave, the natural juices will mix with the Bisto Powder helping to brown the outside and add extra flavour. This applies also to whole chickens and chicken joints, where it is important to achieve an appetising colour. Bisto Powder can also be mixed with wine, soy sauce, lemon juice, Worcestershire sauce, tomato ketchup, or fruit juice, or a combination of any of these, for added interest and flavour. Another way to ensure meat and poultry have a good brown outside is to grill or fry joints quickly on all sides before cooking by microwave. Small cuts of meat like steaks, chops and burgers, as well as sausages, can be cooked in a special browning dish which is first preheated, according to the manufacturer's instructions, and the meat cooked in it in a single layer on its special browning surface.

Combination microwave ovens

These are doubly useful for microwave meat cookery as they combine microwave and conventional cooking in one oven, so meat can be cooked by microwave and browned by conventional heat. Follow the guidelines in the manual accompanying your oven.

The freezer and the microwave

Microwave ovens are particularly beneficial when used in conjunction with a freezer, as not only can food be thawed quickly but dishes can be cooked by microwave, frozen, then defrosted and reheated when needed. The following points are worth bearing in mind if you want to get the best from both appliances:
• Don't rush the process of defrosting either fresh meat or a pre-cooked dish. Follow the suggested times laid down in your microwave manual, increasing or decreasing them as you find necessary.
• Allow food to stand after defrosting, so the internal temperature can even out.
• When freezing cooked meat dishes, choose containers that can be put

back in the microwave when the time comes for defrosting. Also use dishes of a suitable size. For example, if freezing chops in a sauce, the sauce should cover the meat so it will reheat evenly and the sauce won't boil too soon and evaporate.

● When defrosting cooked dishes, break up, stir, turn over and rearrange the food as necessary so you get an evenly-heated result.

● When defrosting uncooked meat, it is advisable to go on and cook it straight away as the meat can easily get hot around the edges and start to cook before defrosting is complete. Break apart chops and burgers as soon as possible so they defrost quicker.

Roasting times for meat and poultry in the microwave

These times are based on a microwave oven with a 650–700 watt output. They should only be taken as a guide and reference to your own microwave manual is recommended. For ovens with a lower output, add a few minutes to the times.

Cut	Time for 500 g (1 lb)	Standing time	Special points
BEEF			
Topside	5 minutes (rare) 6–7 minutes (medium) 8–10 minutes (well done)	15–20 minutes	Cook on full power
Sirloin	5 minutes (rare) 6–7 minutes (medium) 8–10 minutes (well done)	15–30 minutes	Cook on full power
Rib of beef, boned, rolled	6 minutes (rare) 7–8 minutes (medium) 8–10 minutes (well done)	15–30 minutes	Cook on 70% power
LAMB			
Leg or shoulder – on the bone	11 minutes	25–30 minutes	Cook on 70% power
Leg or shoulder – off the bone	11 minutes	25–30 minutes	Cook on 70% power
PORK			
Leg fillet end	12 minutes	30 minutes	Remove crackling, crisp separately under grill. Cook on 70% power
Loin, whole boned and rolled	12 minutes	30 minutes	Cook on 70% power

BACON			
Collar joint	18 minutes	30 minutes	Full power for first 5 minutes, then 50% power
TURKEY			
Whole, stuffed	9–11 minutes	15 minutes	Shield tips of wings and legs with foil. Cook on full power. Turn over 3 or 4 times
Whole, boned and stuffed	10 minutes	15 minutes	Cook on full power. Turn over half-way
Joints	6–8 minutes	10 minutes	Cook on full power, thin parts towards centre
Boneless breasts	2–3 minutes	2 minutes	Cook on full power
CHICKEN			
Whole, stuffed	8–10 minutes	15 minutes	Shield tips of wings and legs with foil. Cook on full power Turn over half-way
Whole, boned and stuffed	10 minutes	15 minutes	Cook on full power. Turn over half-way
Joints	6–8 minutes	10 minutes	Cook on full power, thin parts towards centre
Boneless breasts	2–3 minutes	2 minutes	Cook on full power

Converting a conventional recipe to microwave cooking

If you have a favourite recipe it's usually possible to convert it to cooking by microwave. Bear in mind the following points:

• Cooking by microwave is roughly 3–4 times as fast as cooking by conventional means so reduce cooking times to about one third or a quarter, depending on the recipe. Set the power level according to whether a dish needs fast or slow cooking.

• Substitute non-metallic bowls for saucepans, and shallow dishes or microwave trays with racks, for roasting tins.

• Re-position joints, rearrange small cuts of meat and stir casseroles to ensure even cooking.

- Cut down on the amount of fat used and remember that you can *never* use a microwave oven for deep fat frying.
- Reduce cooking liquids by half to two-thirds, cut meat into even-sized pieces for casseroling and shield thin areas of large joints and poultry.
- Allow for the 'standing time' when calculating the time needed to cook a dish by microwave.

Note: Timings in microwave recipes are based on a 650 watt oven.

ROAST LEG OF LAMB WITH ROSEMARY

Serves 6

*1 small leg of lamb, weighing about
    2 kg (4 lb)
3 or 4 sprigs of fresh rosemary*

*1 clove of garlic, crushed
15 ml (1 tbsp) Bisto Powder
30 ml (2 tbsp) redcurrant jelly*

1. Weigh the leg of lamb and calculate the microwaving time by allowing 11 minutes per 500 g (1 lb).
2. Make small slits in the skin of the lamb with a sharp knife. Lard the slits with rosemary needles and garlic.
3. Blend the Bisto Powder and jelly and brush over the lamb.
4. Wrap a small piece of foil around the thin leg end of the lamb. Place the lamb in a roasting bag and cut a small slit in the bag to allow steam to escape. Stand on a plate or a rack in a shallow dish. Alternatively place the lamb on a rack in a shallow dish and cover it loosely with cling film.
5. Microwave for calculated time at 70% (medium-high), turning the joint over once half-way through the cooking time. Test the lamb to see if it is done to your liking and microwave for a further few minutes if necessary. Cover with foil and leave to stand for 30 minutes before serving.

MINCED BEEF BOLOGNESE

Serves 4   ✱

*500 g (1 lb) lean minced beef
1 onion, chopped finely
60 ml (4 tbsp) tomato purée
397 g (14 oz) can of chopped tomatoes
15 ml (1 tbsp) Bisto Powder
200 ml (7 fl oz) cold water
5 ml (1 tsp) dried marjoram*

*5 ml (1 tsp) dried basil
5 ml (1 tsp) sugar
50 g (2 oz) mushrooms, sliced thinly
100 g (4 oz) salami, cut into 5 mm
    (¼-inch) dice
ground black pepper*

1. Place the beef in a large bowl and break it up with a fork or spoon.
2. Stir in the onion. Microwave uncovered for 5 minutes at 100% (high)

or until the meat is no longer pink, stirring after 3 minutes. Drain off any excess fat.

3. Stir in the tomato purée, chopped tomatoes, Bisto Powder, cold water, marjoram, basil and sugar. Microwave uncovered at 50% (medium) for 30 minutes, until the sauce is thick and pulpy, stirring every 10 minutes.

4. Stir in the mushrooms and salami and season with ground black pepper. Microwave for a further 5 minutes at 50% (medium) and serve spooned over cooked pasta and sprinkled with grated parmesan cheese.

TANGY ROAST BACON

Serves 6

1.5 kg (3 lb) bacon collar joint, soaked overnight in cold water
Glaze:
15 ml (1 tbsp) Bisto Powder
15 ml (1 tbsp) maple-flavoured syrup
45 ml (3 tbsp) sweetened pineapple juice
a pinch of ground cloves

1. Place the bacon joint on a roasting rack in a shallow dish and cover loosely with cling film or kitchen paper.

2. Microwave for 5 minutes at 100% (high). Reduce power output to 50% (medium) and microwave for a further 45 minutes. Remove from oven and cut away the rind from the joint, removing any string as well.

3. To make the glaze: mix together the Bisto Powder, maple-flavoured syrup, pineapple juice and ground cloves. Brush over the bacon. Re-cover and microwave at 50% (medium) for a further 10 minutes.

4. Wrap in foil and leave to stand for 30 minutes.

INDEX

Design and illustrations:
Ken Vail Graphic Design
Photography: Graham Miller
Stylist: Pip Kelly
Home Economist: Maxine Clarke
Typeset by Goodfellow & Egan, Cambridge
Printed and bound by Cayfosa, Barcelona